WADSWORTH PHILOSOPHERS SERIES

ON

GADAMER

Patricia Altenbernd Johnson
University of Dayton

D1568762

Thomson Learning™

Australia • Canada • Denmark • Japan • Mexico • New Zealand • Philippines
Puerto Rico • Singapore • Spain • United Kingdom • United States

Printed in the United States of America
1 2 3 4 5 6 7 03 02 01 00 99

For permission to use material from this text, contact us:
Web: www.thomsonrights.com
Fax: 1-800-730-2215
Phone: 1-800-730-2214

For more information, contact:
Wadsworth/Thomson Learning
10 Davis Drive
Belmont, CA 94002-3098
USA
www.wadsworth.com

ISBN: 0-534-57598-6

Contents

1

Apprenticeships

Hans-Georg Gadamer was born on February 11, 1900. On the title page of *Philosophical Apprenticeships*, an intellectual autobiography published in 1977, Gadamer writes *De nobis ipsis silemus,* "I want to be quiet about myself." This quietness is in keeping with his insistence on the need for philosophy in the twentieth century to move away from the Cartesian emphasis on self-consciousness. Rather than base all understanding on the individual human self as a foundation, Gadamer emphasizes the dialogical nature of philosophy and of human existence. He emphasizes that humans are far more formed by tradition, and by what Cartesian philosophy views as prejudices, than by individual choices. Who we are is to a great extent influenced by those others around us who challenge us to act and to reflect on our actions. Because of this emphasis, Gadamer gives an account of his own life in terms of apprenticeships. As an apprentice, he is a beginner, one who is learning in relationship to others. Gadamer's account of his life, in *Philosophical Apprenticeships* and in the introduction that he writes for Volume XXIV of The Library of Living Philosophers, traces his journey through the twentieth century as the development of the ability to engage in philosophical conversation. A brief look at his life and apprenticeships is a helpful introduction to his thought

Beginning To Think

Gadamer's childhood was spent in Breslau. He came to maturity during the First World War, but lived far from the fronts and the strongest impact of the war. In his brief accounts of his childhood, he reports that he was interested in the Prussian military tradition with its efficiency and discipline. People thought he would become an officer. He recounts his memory of a family discussion of the sinking of the *Titanic*. Gadamer's father compared the event to the destruction of an entire village of people. His response to his father was that they were just farmers. He remembers the lesson he learned in apologizing to their maid who was from the country. Perhaps this was an initial event in his life when he began to recognize that understanding takes place in conversation with others.

Gadamer's interests in theater and poetry quickly turned him from a military direction. He read Shakespeare and lyric poetry. He was influenced by Thomas Mann's *Observations of an Unpolitical Person* and by the novels of Hermann Hesse. Much to his father's disappointment, he turned to the humanities. His father was a natural scientist and could not understand his son's love of the human sciences. Gadamer began University studies at eighteen, and his parents' influence began to diminish.

Early in his academic career, he read *Europe and Asia* by Theodor Lessing. While he now judges this work to be second-rate, he acknowledges that it still had a revolutionary effect on him as a young man. The book called into question his previous cultural understanding. He says that it relativized his world and at the same time enabled him to begin to think. He moved away from his parent's political positions and engaged in political rhetoric that embraced democratic-republican language. He read Kierkegaard's *Either/Or* and began to reflect on the nature of history. During a vacation, he found Kant's *Critique of Pure Reason* in his father's library. He reports, "I really brooded over the book, but not the slightest understandable thought slipped out of it" (PA 5). Nevertheless, this was the beginning of a lifetime of philosophical conversations.

Studies at Marburg

Gadamer's interest in philosophy motivated him to study in Marburg in 1919. This was a period of philosophical and theological development, and Marburg was alive with ideas. The theologian Karl Barth had just published his *Commentary on the Letter to the Romans*, and what was to become known as dialectical theology was beginning. The influence of Nietzsche was also beginning to be important, influencing advocates of life-philosophy. Husserl's new phenomenological method was discussed. This method challenged the orientation of philosophy towards scientific facts. Husserl questioned the scientific theory of knowledge of the day and put phenomenological description in its place. Students and faculty read Wilhelm Dilthey and Ernst Troeltsch and talked about the issue of historical relativism and the importance of the world of lived experience. Stefan George, the poet, was part of an academic circle that critiqued culture.

Gadamer reports on this circle of intellectuals who were close friends with Stephan George. Students were either part of the group or they were outsiders. Gadamer was an outsider; yet, when he contracted polio in 1922, Friedrich Wolters, the center of this group, was one of the first to visit him. Gadamer's life was already focused on conversation. Despite his illness, he remembers the subject matter of that conversation. They picked up on something Paul Natorp had said in a lecture and discussed the dangers of individuation and individuality. Gadamer notes that the "George Circle embodied a corporate consciousness at a high spiritual level at a time when society was atomizing" (PA 9).

Gadamer studied with Natorp at Marburg and was deeply impressed with Natorp's artistic and mystical tendencies. Gadamer tells the story of Natorp lecturing during a power failure and continuing with the light of a candle. Natorp emphasized system and methodology. He used the candle to symbolize his position that even when the whole unified light system goes out, the mystical candle can still illuminate truth. From Natorp, Gadamer also learned the importance of silence. If there was nothing to be said, then there was silence. This silence did not have to be filled up with idle conversation. But, it could be used for the reading of poetry. Gadamer remembers that Natorp particularly loved to read the dramas of Rabindranath Tagore, a great writer from India. Once Tagore came to Marburg and Natorp and Tagore sat side-by-side on a podium. Gadamer remembers them as "both men of deep inwardness and convincing presence" (PA

3

11). Natorp supervised Gadamer's doctoral dissertation on Plato. At the time, Gadamer thought Natorp was rigorous, even though he allowed Gadamer to complete the work at the young age of twenty-two. Later when Gadamer directed students in thesis work and they complained of his rigor, he had his wife read the dissertation that he had written under Natorp's supervision. She assured him that he would never have accepted the dissertation!

Nicolai Hartman also influenced the philosophy students at Marburg. Hartman held evening conversations with students, beginning at about seven and lasting until after midnight. They played a game called "teakettle" where they formulated riddles that seemed to have simple yes or no answers, but that were actually full of ambiguity. Hartmann's evening conversations were cut short when Martin Heidegger began presenting lectures at seven in the morning. It may be difficult for contemporary students to understand an intellectual excitement so intense as to get students to class so early in the morning. Gadamer explains the importance of Heidegger as,

> *A basic event, not only for me but for all of the Marburg of those days. He demonstrated a well-integrated spiritual energy laced with such a plain power of verbal expression and such a radical simplicity of questions that the habitual and more or less mastered games of wit and categories or modalities quickly left me.* (PA 19)

Gadamer went to Freiburg in the summer of 1923 to study with Heidegger. He reports that it was that summer that he began to learn the importance of embracing questions, especially alien questions.

Life as a Dozent

Gadamer worked in Marburg from 1924-1938. He first served as a teaching assistant to Heidegger along with Gerhard Krüger and Karl Löwith. In the German educational system, students who want to have permanent positions as university faculty assist faculty with permanent positions. This system is an apprenticeship system. The professor mentors students through what is called a habilitation. At the end of this period, the student is ready to become a *Dozent*. Gadamer's habilitation was celebrated in 1928 after Heidegger had left Marburg.

Gadamer remained at Marburg as a *Dozent*. This position is like that of an assistant professor in the United States, but does not pay nearly so well. Much of the salary is based on tuition money from students who enroll for advertised lectures. As a *Dozent*, Gadamer gave lectures on a range of topics. He reports that he was a very shy lecturer and that rather than clarify issues, he tended to show all of the confusions involved in them. His friends invented a measure that they called the "Gad." This "designated a settled measure of unnecessary complications" (PA 71).

A *Dozent* learns to teach by teaching and by engaging in research. This process is based in the belief that at a certain point in education, one knows when one does not know something and has the tools to learn it. Once something is learned, the learning can be passed on. Gadamer acknowledges that it took him a good deal of time to become a teacher. He writes of that period, "But what an adventure it was to be always applying oneself to new themes and new objects" (PA 73). By 1933, Gadamer had reached a point in his career when it was appropriate for him to receive a job offer. But the rise of Hitler and National Socialism changed these expectations. Gadamer had been focused on learning and teaching and on the conversations with colleagues. He writes of the events of 1933,

> *It was a terrible awakening, and we could not absolve ourselves of having failed to perform adequately as citizens. We had underrated Hitler and his kind...It was a widespread conviction in intellectual circles that Hitler in coming to power would deconstruct the nonsense he had used to drum up the movement, and we counted the anti-Semitism as part of this nonsense.* (PA 75)

Hitler's rhetoric did not deconstruct, and the situations in the universities became difficult and divisive. Students and faculty were expected to salute, Jewish intellectuals were forced to leave the universities, and university constitutions were changed.

At Marburg, Rudolf Bultmann continued to facilitate academic presentations and conversations. These had to be carried out with caution and indirect language. Gadamer reports that Bultmann gave a presentation on "The Light." Gadamer presented on Plato and the poets and began with the words of Goethe,

> *Difficult though it might be to detect it, a certain polemical thread runs through any philosophical writing. He who philosophizes is not at one with the previous and contemporary world's ways of thinking of things. Thus Plato's discussions are often not only*

5

directed to something but also against it. (DD 39)

Gadamer decided to try to save his academic life while not making political commitments that would force him to betray friends. He did not want to become a martyr. He did not want to leave Germany.

In these difficult political times, Gadamer took a "rehabilitation" course. This course was conducted at a camp that was directed by a man who tried to remain aloof from Nazism. He did not demand political lip service, although the physical exercises and nationalistic singing and games were required. Gadamer made contacts at the camp with many "comrades." These people became friends and enabled him to get a faculty position at Leipzig.

Leipzig

As a professor in Leipzig, Gadamer was expected to teach the full range of the history of philosophy. He took a textual approach to teaching and avoided all political discussions in the classroom. While his teaching could not be easily connected to his research, he was able to do seminars on Husserl. He also taught Rilke, who was the poet of the academic resistance. He remembers teaching Rilke's third elegy in the *Duino Elegies* in the dark, by candle light after the terribly destructive bombing of Leipzig in 1943.

Students were questioned about faculty activity and even served as informants. Gadamer reports that he once used as a logical example, the claim "All asses are brown." A woman student repeated this example to a friend. Gadamer was called before the rector, who concluded that the example was intended as a logical, not a political, one. The student did not fare so well. She was removed from the University and put to work in a factory.

Gadamer published very little during the war years. In 1934, he published "Plato and the Poets," the paper that he gave for the Bultmann group. In 1942, he published "Plato's Educational State." He reports that this article was written as a "kind of alibi" (Hahn 13). The German universities were able to survive the war because the sciences were needed. The humanities and social sciences survived insofar as they connected themselves to this war effort. Gadamer avoided contributing to anti-Semitic writing, by focusing on the classical philology that he had studied while at Marburg. He also published a monograph in 1942, *People and History in the Thinking of*

6

Herder. This monograph was a study of the concept of power in Herder's historical thinking. The work gained him some undesired attention, even though he was careful to avoid contemporary implications. He presented the monograph as a lecture to French officers at a camp for prisoners of war and told them that "an empire that extends itself beyond measure" is "near its fall" (Hahn 14). In general, however, he took few political risks and worked to enable the university to survive with some intellectual integrity in tact. He says of those times,

> *I saw my task as a teacher in strengthening the courage of the German academic youth to think for themselves and to strengthen their own sense of judgment. This means first of all engaging in the primacy of dialogue in the theory and practice of teaching. In this way we researchers and teachers have to obey the law of the long breath in the field of politics.* (Hahn 258)

Because he did manage to avoid Nazi ties during the war, during the American occupation of Leipzig, he became Rector. The American presence was replaced by Russian control. In this situation, Gadamer had to become political. He learned about politics inside and outside of the universities. He says that what he "learned above all was the unfruitfulness and impossibility of all restorative thinking" (PA 104). He also learned the political value of openness. Since the Russians were distrustful, he was always available to them and "confronted them with absolute openness and with decisively clear opposition" (PA 107). He helped other colleagues find and go to positions that would ensure their freedom. He was arrested once, but only after having made the decision to take a position at Frankfurt am Main. Having convinced the Russians that his decision to go to Frankfurt was based on love of his own country and its literature, he left Leipzig in 1947.

Heidelberg

After two years in Frankfurt, he assumed Karl Jaspers' chair at Heidelberg. In 1949, he was finally able to return to teaching and turn to his own scholarship. Gadamer found students eager to learn and to develop as philosophers. He followed the model of Hartmann and established a small group of students and faculty who met regularly at his home to discuss philosophical texts. He also introduced regular guest lecturers into the curriculum. He tells the story of one lecture given by Jean Hyppolite, a French intellectual and translator of Hegel. Hyppolite refused to speak or hear spoken the word "Europe." Hyppolite thought that a belief in Europe implied an imperialist position.

Gadamer convinced Karl Löwith to return to Germany and to take a position at Heidelberg. There was a renewed interest in Heidegger's thought, and Löwith opposed Heidegger's later thought, calling it mythology. Gadamer disagreed, seeing Heidegger's thought as needed thinking. Yet, Gadamer and Löwith worked together to teach a seminar on Heidegger's "On the Essence of Truth." Gadamer continued his dedication to developing meaningful dialogue. He was developing his teaching as hermeneutic practice. In conjunction with this work, he and Helmut Kuhn founded the *Philosophical Rundschau*, a journal devoted to critique. Käte Gadamer-Lekebusch oversaw this journal for many years.

Teaching and then administrative duties as Dean of the faculty of philosophy consumed Gadamer's time during the academic year. His summers were devoted to writing based on what he was learning through his teaching. Through teaching and research, Gadamer developed philosophical hermeneutics. His major work, *Truth and Method* was published in 1960.

Retirement Years

Gadamer published his major philosophical work late in his teaching career. Retirement then gave him the opportunity to travel and to present and develop his ideas on philosophical hermeneutics. He improved his spoken English as he met with students in the United States and Canada. He lectured to students in theology, literature, and philology, as well as philosophy. *Truth and Method* remains the basis for his thought, but he has continued to develop philosophical hermeneutics and some of the concepts that are fundamental to his thinking. Gadamer is a major philosopher in the twentieth century. Not only has he experienced many of the major events of this century first hand, he has also articulated a philosophical approach that emphasizes the importance of conversation for human self-understanding, both individual and communal.

2

Philosophical Hermeneutics

When Gadamer was preparing the manuscript for *Truth and Method* for publication, he proposed that the title of the book be *Philosophical Hermeneutics*. His publishers thought that this would not mean anything to his readers, and so the term "philosophical hermeneutics" was placed in the subtitle. For a reader new to Gadamer's work and to this general area of philosophical thought, the term "hermeneutics" is sometimes still confusing. The word has its origin in the Greek word that means "to interpret" and is connected to the name of the Greek god, Hermes. While Hermes was considered a trickster, he was also credited with discovering language and writing. He was the messenger of the gods. In this role, he carried messages from the sphere of the gods to humans. He translated divine communication into a form that humans could understand.

A brief historical account of hermeneutics is helpful for understanding Gadamer's thought. The developments of Friedrich Schleiermacher, Wilhelm Dilthey, and Martin Heidegger are all important for Gadamer's work.

Schleiermacher

Until the work of Friedrich Schleiermacher (1768-1834) in the early 1800's, there were diverse, specialized hermeneutics. These

9

hermeneutics were methodologies for interpreting various types of texts, particularly literary, religious, and legal texts. Schleiermacher believes that underlying all of these particular hermeneutics, there is a general hermeneutics. He recognizes that there are differences in the various disciplines. They examine different types of texts and find different issues to be most important. Nevertheless, Schleiermacher maintains that understanding does not take place in isolated, or discipline specific occurrences. Understanding law and understanding religion require the exercise of a common human understanding. Schleiermacher maintains that children learn and practice hermeneutics, the art of understanding, as they come to understand the meaning of words.

Schleiermacher proposes to set out the principles of hermeneutics as this art of general understanding. The principles are not a methodology that will guarantee correct understanding. They are guidelines for practicing the art of understanding. While he believes that all humans are able to understand others, he also recognizes that some are better at doing this than others. Everyone can easily relate examples of misunderstandings. It is also easy to identify people who are good listeners. The principles of Schleiermacher's hermeneutics are an attempt to recognize and follow the ways of understanding of the most gifted listeners and conversationalists.

Schleiermacher's hermeneutics distinguishes two types, or moments, of understanding. He calls one grammatical and the other psychological. Grammatical understanding focuses on the language or words that are used. This type of understanding requires a person to know the language that is spoken and to have a grasp of the totality of that language. Once a language is learned, this moment of understanding is usually taken for granted. The general assumption that understanding takes place is occasionally challenged. In classroom situations, a teacher may assume that students understand what is being said only to discover on an examination that words or concepts are in truth very confusing to the class. A good teacher develops the ability to recognize when a class does not understand. A good student develops the ability to raise questions as part of the process of understanding.

For Schleiermacher, hermeneutics is the art of understanding at this grammatical level, but it is also a psychological art. Hermeneutics is the art of moving inside the thought of another person and understanding that thought from the person's perspective. Sometimes this is called understanding the author's intent. This psychological art most interested Schleiermacher. He outlines a divinatory method based on the contention that the common structure of all humanity is such that

10

one individual contains elements of all others. A person can understand another person through a process of self-understanding. Psychological hermeneutics develops the capabilities of one person to stand in another's position, to transform oneself into that other person. This approach is an attempt to understand what that person means. It is grasping the inwardness of another mind.

Schleiermacher also uses what he terms a comparative method to develop understanding. In the comparative method, several authors are placed in comparison and so a broader understanding is gained. In trying to understand a text, one must try to enter the mind of the author by the divinatory method. But this needs to be complemented with the comparative method. Schleiermacher develops what is sometimes called the hermeneutical circle. Understanding occurs by focusing on small parts and then placing them in the larger context. Each step changes the total meaning and adds to the fullness of understanding.

Schleiermacher's hermeneutics is important for Gadamer because it recognizes that the task of hermeneutics as universal. However, Gadamer notes that Schleiermacher's starting point for developing his hermeneutics was theology. Because of this, he focuses on texts such as the *Bible*, whose authority is not disputed. Gadamer finds this a significant limitation. He writes,

> *His hermeneutical theory was still a long way from a historiography that could serve as a methodological organon for the human sciences. Its goal was the exact understanding of particular texts, which was to be aided by the universal character of historical contexts. This is Schleiermacher's limitation, and the historical worldview had to move beyond it.* (TM 197)

The work of Dilthey makes this historical move.

Dilthey

Wilhelm Dilthey (1833-1911) is deeply influenced by Schleiermacher, devoting a portion of his own writing to a biography of Schleiermacher. Dilthey believes that hermeneutics holds the possibility of establishing a science of understanding that can provide a methodological foundation for the human sciences (*Geisteswissenschaften*). Disciplines such as history and literature that study things that are created by humans can have an epistemology, a way of distinguishing true from false knowledge, in a way analogous to the natural sciences.

In developing this methodological hermeneutics, Dilthey distinguishes explanation and understanding. He defines explanation as the method of the natural sciences. It deals with the outer manifestations of things. Explanation deals with a particular thing only as a manifestation of a type and not in its inner individuality. Understanding grasps the individual in its inner and outer forms. Explanation and understanding are methods that can be used to approach the same thing. The thing does not determine the appropriateness of one method or the other. What is important is the context. Explanation is appropriate when something is approached as an object of nature. Understanding is appropriate when something, perhaps the same thing, is approached as an expression of life.

Medicine helps to illustrate the distinction that Dilthey makes. When a person is ill, a physician uses the science of medicine to diagnose and prescribe. The person's symptoms are understood as symptoms that any human body exhibits when attached by a specific disease. Certain forms of treatment are appropriate against that disease. If someone has a very sore throat and a positive test for strep, then a course of antibiotics is the correct treatment. In this treatment, the person is treated as a type—someone who has a strep infection. But the same physician may also use the method of understanding in practicing medicine as an art. A physician can come to know his or her patients as individuals. If the person with the infection is a frightened child, the physician may know how to help that individual child relax and cope with the illness. Gadamer remarks that,

> *Doctors must be able to look beyond the 'case' they are treating and have regard for the human being as a whole in that person's particular life situation. Indeed doctors must even be capable of reflecting on their own medical intervention and its probable effect on the patient.* (EH 42-43)

For Schleiermacher, intuition and feeling are the means for entering the inner aspects of human life. These are introspective approaches. Dilthey rejects this approach and stresses historicality. Humans are temporal, historical, beings. Humans understand themselves in terms of a past and a future and in terms of what they create. The concepts such as cause and effect that explain natural phenomena are not appropriate for understanding human life. In order to understand human life, the concepts employed must be appropriate to this temporal nature. This emphasis on historicality is a move beyond Schleiermacher's hermeneutics and is of fundamental importance for Gadamer's thought.

In conjunction with his emphasis on historicality, Dilthey emphasizes that human life is objectified. Humans create things and so express their inner experience. Dilthey views these human creations as expressions of life, not simply of individual feeling. The way to understand humanity is to focus on expressions of lived experience. Dilthey sees works of art, particularly those that use the form of language, as giving the fullest expression to the inner human life. A work of art does not so much express a particular artist as it expresses a social and historical reality. When we understand a work of art, we understand human life and we understand ourselves.

Dilthey advanced hermeneutics beyond Schleiermacher's psychological focus by considering the importance of historical experience. Gadamer notes that he still "conceives inquiring into the historical past *as deciphering and not as historical experience*" (TM 241). Nevertheless, Dilthey prepared the way for the thought of both Heidegger and Gadamer.

Heidegger

Martin Heidegger (1889-1976) trained in theology and so was familiar with Schleiermacher's thought. He had also studied Dilthey's work. Schleiermacher set out to develop a general theory of hermeneutics but could not overcome the issue of psychologism. Dilthey addressed this problem by emphasizing historicality. Yet, Dilthey retained a distinction between explanation and understanding and so limited understanding to the human sciences and to a method of deciphering.

Heidegger takes a further step in *Being and Time*. Understanding is a basic constituent of the way in which humans are in the world. Understanding is not simply a method for grasping psychological or historical meaning; it is the way that humans exist in the world. Every act of interpretation, scientific or humanistic, is based in human understanding. For Heidegger, understanding is ontological; it is an integral part of human being.

Understanding is the aspect of human being that enables us to transcend ourselves, to move outside of ourselves. This movement is not Schleiermacher's movement of one mind into another. Nor is it

13

Dilthey's life expression where the inner moves to an outer communal form. It is a movement of grasping our own possibilities and of becoming what we are. In *Being and Time*, Heidegger develops a detailed analysis of human existence and calls this analysis a hermeneutic.

As a student of Heidegger, Gadamer was deeply influenced by his approach to philosophizing. He takes Heidegger's main achievement to be recognizing that understanding is the original character of human life. In explaining Heidegger, he emphasizes that whenever a person understands, that person understands him or herself and looks at possibilities as possibilities for him or herself. In Heidegger's thought, "the structure of historical understanding appears with its full ontological background" (TM 261).

Gadamer does not incorporate all of Heidegger's analysis of human existence into his own hermeneutics, nor does he use the vocabulary that Heidegger develops. Indeed, Gadamer thought that those who adopted this vocabulary often ran the risk of missing Heidegger's primary contributions. Yet, Gadamer begins his development of hermeneutics with Heidegger's analysis of understanding. He proposes to demonstrate how this insight is also "expressed in the understanding of historical tradition" (TM 264). This is the task that Gadamer develops in his philosophical hermeneutics.

Philosophical Hermeneutics

Heidegger's *Being and Time* was published in 1927. Gadamer did not publish *Truth and Method* until 1960. However, the years between these two publications were years in which Gadamer developed his philosophical hermeneutics. In his intellectual autobiography, Gadamer says that during those years he taught hermeneutic practice.

As a teacher, Gadamer was concerned to help students develop the art of understanding and of making something understandable to others. In his work on Greek philosophy and in his teaching, he focused on the history of concepts. All of this work was hermeneutics in its practical form. Philosophical hermeneutics looks at this practice from a theoretical perspective. He explains this in his essay "Hermeneutics as Practical Philosophy,"

Hermeneutics has to do with a theoretical attitude towards the

14

> *practice of interpretation, the interpretation of texts, but also in relation to the experiences interpreted in them and in our communicatively unfolded orientations in the world. This theoretic stance only makes us aware reflectively of what is performatively at play in the practical experience of understanding.* (RAS 112)

Gadamer emphasizes that the practice of understanding and theoretical reflection on that practice are inseparable. As one practices understanding, one is in a better position to reflect on what it is to be a being who understands. As one reflects on such universal questions, one is in a better position to practice the art of understanding. Insofar as humans understand and reflect on the process of understanding, they are inclined towards philosophy.

In developing philosophical hermeneutics, Gadamer focuses on a number of concepts. These enable him to develop his practice of and theoretical reflection on understanding and serve as the defining concepts of his work. By looking at concepts of aesthetic and historical consciousness, he emphasizes the need for contemporary humans to overcome the primacy of the concept of self-consciousness and to reexamine the concepts of tradition and prejudice. He identifies linguisticality as a concept that can help develop an understanding of what it is to be a human being. Chapters Three, Four, and Five explore his use of these concepts in the development of philosophical hermeneutics in its most theoretical form. Readers new to philosophy or to philosophical hermeneutics may find these chapters complex. Chapters Six, Seven, and Eight focus on the more practical aspects of Gadamer's thought. It is important to understand both the theoretical and practical aspects of Gadamer's work. However, some readers may find it helpful to turn to sections in the last three chapters and then return to Chapters Three, Four, and Five. Either approach to understanding Gadamer's philosophical hermeneutics is in keeping with his belief that theory and practice ought not be viewed as separate activities.

3

The Experience of Art

Gadamer begins his studies on hermeneutics from the experience of art and from the experience of historical tradition. In each case, he examines the experiences in order to address the alienation that characterizes twentieth-century human existence. This alienation is our inheritance from the Enlightenment. In emphasizing reason and the foundational importance of self-consciousness, the Enlightenment distanced humans from experiences that enable us to understand our existence. It sets a distance between the subject and object and then makes overcoming that distance into a problem. Gadamer argues that these developments in philosophy restrict truth to scientific and conceptual knowledge. Gadamer challenges this. He believes that the work of art also possesses truth. Recognizing this places both art and history in a new light. It also helps humans begin to overcome alienation. Understanding art helps humans to better understand and embrace who they are.   Philosophy is then able to overcome the dichotomous thinking that poses subject over against object.

Some of the language that Gadamer uses in developing his reflections may appear complex, especially to readers who do not have a background in continental philosophy of the twentieth century. Yet, in many respects, Gadamer's ideas are clearly illustrated by everyday life experiences. For example, when a person sets out on a career path, he or she has an idea, a concept, of what it is to be a member of that profession. A person who wants to be a teacher has an idea of what it is to be a teacher. But at the beginning, the future teacher is very distant from what it is to be a teacher. The truth of being a teacher can only be understood through the process of teaching. In the process of becoming a teacher, one may embrace a particular concept of what this means. For example, a teacher may conceptualize him or herself as the one who always knows the answer. If, in the process of becoming a teacher, this concept is retained, alienation occurs. The experience of teaching and the concept of what it is to be a teacher do not correspond. The person who desires to be a teacher has not achieved the ideal, and so holds that he or she is not a good teacher or a real teacher. The truth is that the person may be a good teacher; the problem is with the inadequacy of the concept of what it is to be a teacher.

Gadamer believes that we are alienated because our concept of what it is to be human does not correspond to our lived experience as humans. If we have a better concept of what it is to be a human being, we will be able to overcome this alienation and live fuller human lives. Reflections on the experiences of art and of history provide Gadamer with a starting point for developing philosophical hermeneutics and for the practical task of overcoming alienation. This chapter examines his work on the experience of art. Chapter 4 addresses the experience of history.

Aesthetic Consciousness

From his earliest interest in philosophy, Gadamer has been concerned with the relation of the experience of art to philosophy. This concern has remained central to his thought throughout the century of his life. He believes that correctly connecting the experience of art with philosophy is one of the most important tasks of contemporary thought. Gadamer's critique of the concept of aesthetic consciousness not only provides the starting point for understanding philosophical hermeneutics; it also exemplifies his philosophical approach. He begins with a very thorough analysis of the contemporary concept. He uses a dialectical method, comparing that concept with the lived experience of art. Finally, he articulates a rehabilitated concept. This process of rehabilitation of the concept involves two aspects. Gadamer goes back to the origins of the concept prior to Cartesian and Enlightenment thought. Often for Gadamer, this is a return to Greek thought, especially the thought of Plato. Gadamer shows the heritage, usually overlooked, that is still part of the contemporary concept. He shows how our use of the concept does not escape its heritage. Yet, a rehabilitated concept is also a new concept; it is made new without being divorced from its origins.

Critique of Aesthetic Consciousness

Gadamer's critique maintains that the concept of aesthetic consciousness that has dominated the twentieth century is a relatively new concept, having its roots in Enlightenment thought, particularly in Kant. In most contemporary thinking about art, people approach art as a form of perceptual enjoyment. This aesthetic consciousness enjoys the sensuous form, but the experience is separated from other types of experience. Gadamer terms this move 'aesthetic differentiation.' Art in its various manifestations is understood as contributing to the life of feeling, but not to human knowledge or truth. Because of this, aesthetic consciousness is treated as purely subjective. Gadamer writes,

> *Thus through 'aesthetic differentiation' the work loses its place and the world to which it belongs insofar as it belongs instead to aesthetic consciousness. Correlatively, the artist too loses his place in the world.* (TM 87)

Art and the artist are viewed as making no ultimately important contribution to society. Art provides pleasure but does not bring new knowledge.

Attitudes in contemporary American society towards painting and poetry both help exemplify Gadamer's point. Most people do not fill their homes and living spaces with original art. Paintings that are considered great art by those who have the best developed taste, or aesthetic consciousness, are usually housed in museums. People go to museums to experience the art. Not only is the art placed in a separate space from everyday life, it is also viewed as atemporal. Gadamer says that these collections actually conceal the fact that they grew out of collections of contemporary work. The role of art is simply to elicit feeling. This art may sell for millions of dollars, but its value is simply as a commodity. Possession of great art is an indication of wealth. We do not expect art to provide us with knowledge.

Poetry is even more fully devalued in American society. Poets are not widely read, and many people consider themselves able poets. This judgment is based in the idea that poetry is simply the expression of feeling. If feeling is expressed, then the work is called poetry. As a

18

result, a poet can seldom earn a living writing poetry. A poet is not seen as a prophet or as contributing to the conceptual knowledge of society.

This approach to art results in the separation of aesthetic experience from other forms of experience. Science and scientific method are understood as the only realm of knowledge. Gadamer asks, "But is it right to reserve the concept of truth for conceptual knowledge? Must we not also admit that the work of art possesses truth?" (TM 41-42).

The Experience of Art

Gadamer maintains that this way of conceptualizing aesthetic consciousness is shown to be limited when we actually examine our experience of art and when we look at the ways in which other historical periods have conceptualized art. He says, "we discover that from the classical period up to the age of the baroque art was dominated by quite other standards of value than that of being experienced, and thus our eyes are opened to totally unfamiliar artistic worlds" (TM 71). Gadamer's review leads him to the recognition that in other periods, people surrounded themselves with art that served religious and secular functions. They did not adopt an aesthetic attitude towards these works. They lived with them and understood them.

Gadamer describes the experience of a work of art as an encounter with a world. If we are able to suspend the point of view of aesthetic consciousness that requires us to remain distant from a work of art, we can enter into the work of art. When we do this, we enter into a world. He says, "The pantheon of art is not a timeless present that presents itself to a pure aesthetic consciousness, but the act of a mind and spirit that has collected and gathered itself historically" (TM 97). When we enter the world of the work of art, we are able to understand ourselves and our world through the work of art. Gadamer holds that this is self-understanding which only occurs when we encounter something other than the self. Self-understanding includes "the unity and integrity of the other." The experience of art contains truth. This truth may be different than the truth of science, but it is not inferior to that truth.

Film provides an example of encountering a work of art. When the viewer enters a theater to watch a film, he or she enters the world of the film. While the viewer may remain distant from the world of the film and focus on the cinematographic elements of the film, this approach misses the full meaning of the film. A film pulls the viewer in and challenges the viewer to participate in the world of the film. Leaving a film, the viewer recognizes that he or she has encountered a world. While this world is never fully the viewer's own world, neither is it totally alien. In experiencing this world, the viewer understands the world encountered and also develops self-understanding.

A Rehabilitated Concept of Art

Gadamer's critique of aesthetic consciousness and his examination of the historical and lived dimensions of the experience of art, lead him to suggest that truth is encountered in the work of art. Art is not simply subjective, having to do with a person's own feeling about something. Understanding takes place in this encounter. This understanding is not the grasping by a subject of something objective. It is not a having or a possessing. The truth of the experience of art is something that we belong to; it catches us. In order to explicate the way in which art overcomes the dichotomy between subject and object, Gadamer's conceptualization of art focuses on the play structure of art.

Play (Spiel)

The concept of play is one of the defining concepts of Gadamer's thought. He develops this concept in relationship to art, but it is central to much of the rest of *Truth and Method.* Play, more than any other of Gadamer's concepts, enables him to understand the dynamic of human existence. He describes play in the following manner,

> *When we speak of play in reference to the experience of art, this means neither the orientation nor even the state of mind of the creator or of those enjoying the work of art, nor the freedom of a subjectivity engaged in play, but the mode of being of the work of art itself.* (TM101)

If play is not an attitude or activity or state of mind of the person, but rather the mode of being of the work of art, then questions arise: What is this mode of being? How does the person who experiences art fit into this play?

Gadamer says that the mode of being, which is play, is primarily a medial one. Play is constituted neither by the object, the work of art, nor by the subject, the artist or appreciator. The play of art draws both of these into itself and is the "to-and-fro movement that is not tied to any goal that brings it to an end" (TM 103). The one who plays certainly enters the play with an attitude; but rather than constituting the play, that attitude is filled and directed by the play itself. Play serves two purposes in Gadamer's work at this point. It is an image for understanding the experience of art, and it exemplifies the possibility for human existence of recognizing that the subject/object dichotomy is not the only, or the most fundamental, way to understand human existence.

Children's play serves as a good example for illustrating Gadamer's point. Most children play games in which they become imaginary characters. Often they devise and wear costumes for these characters. These games have no serious purpose, and yet children are very serious in the play. Children lose themselves in their play. They do not objectify the play and hold it at a distance. They are absorbed in the play. They are no longer themselves, a subject. They act differently than themselves. There is a type of freedom in this play. Children who are taken up in play have a lightness about them. The burdens of life are lifted. Yet, play also places limitations on the children. Play has rules, even if those rules tend to change in the course of the play. Play is also self-representation. Gadamer says that in "spending oneself on the task of the game, one is, in fact, playing oneself out" (TM 108). Children are representing themselves, and in representing, children are representing for someone. There is an audience.

In art, "the closed world of play lets down one of its walls" (TM 108). But Gadamer emphasizes that art does not thereby become an object for an audience. Gadamer uses theater as an example. In English, too, this is a play. The actors on a stage are absorbed in the play. As for the children, play for the actors is self-representation. But it is also representation for an audience. It is not the lack of a wall that makes this representation the case. Rather, Gadamer says, "Openness towards the spectator is part of the closedness of the play. The audience only completes what the play as such is*"* (TM 109). Both the actors and the spectators are part of the play. Gadamer says that both are required to attend to the meaningfulness of the play.

Play is important to human existence, because it is perfected in art. Gadamer says this is a transformation into structure. Transformation is not simply change. It is not that when children grow up they cease to play the games they played as children and instead play bridge or golf. Transformation is total change. When a person is transformed, he or she becomes a different person. Gadamer says, "Thus the transformation into a structure means that what existed previously exists no longer. But also what now exists, what represents itself in the play of art, is the lasting and true" (TM 111). This transformation that takes place in art, is transformation into the true. In the play that is art, what is hidden is brought into the light. The world of the work of art is a transformed world. Through the work of art "everyone recognizes that that is how things are" (TM 113). In the work of art, we recognize truth in that we know and recognize ourselves.

Gadamer emphasizes that recognition is not simply acknowledging something that is familiar. In recognition, what we know is illuminated. It is known as something. The simple example of recognizing a friend illustrates this. There is joy in seeing a familiar form and suddenly knowing, "That is my friend." Art represents truth in such a way that truth is illuminated; it is brought out. Religious art and ritual demonstrate most clearly what Gadamer is pointing out. The art and ritual are essential to the religious truth. The ritual belongs to the world of the religion and only really exists when it is carried out.

This is true of drama and music. They exist to be played and achieve their fullness in being played. Gadamer characterizes this mediated structure as aesthetic non-differentiation. Art is not abstracted out of time as aesthetic consciousness suggests. "The aesthetic attitude is more than it knows of itself" (TM 116). The aesthetic consciousness belongs to what it takes to be its object. It is part of the event, part of the process through which the world of the art, the play, comes to be. This insight leads Gadamer to examine the temporality of art.

Power of Fusion

In "The Festive Character of Theater" (RB), Gadamer speaks of the experience of art as demonstrating what he calls the power of fusion. Art has a radical temporal structure, such that it can elevate the past into the present, not simply as history, but as presence. This means that art has the ability to always be something different. Both repetition and contemporaneity characterize this temporal structure. The work of art is always the same work of art, but it is also always present in the contemporary world.

22

Gadamer illustrates this structure with the example of a festival that is celebrated. Each celebration is a repetition. Religious festivals or celebrations provide good examples. These festivals are repeated on a regular basis. Some, like Christmas, occur once each year. Others, like lighting the Sabbath candles, are far more frequent. Each celebration is neither a new festival nor a remembrance of an earlier festival. Gadamer says of festivals that their "original essence is always to be something different" (TM 123). The temporal structure of the festival is not just repetition; it is contemporaneity. Each celebration is Christmas; it is the Sabbath. For the festival to be contemporaneous is for it to claim the participants and to confront them with their own identity.

The temporal structure of art is such that the work of art does not take us into a past world. The work of art is able to be contemporaneous with every age. The experience of art presents us with the truth of our world, especially our religious and moral world, and enables us to recognize ourselves. In the work of art, we are both self-forgetful and mediated.

Implications of the Rehabilitation of Art

Gadamer's analysis of aesthetic consciousness and his use of the concept of play are not primarily intended to develop a new aesthetic theory, although they have been and can be used in this manner. He uses the experience of art to show us something about ourselves. We are not alienated from the world of our experience. We belong to that world in an integral way. Just as the spectator at the play is part of the event, we are part of the world of our experience. Just as the spectator cannot control the play, so we are not in control of the world. Yet, the spectator interprets the play and so is essential to the meaningfulness of the play. In the rehabilitated concept of art that Gadamer develops, we discover that we are bound to a common historical world.

Gadamer's treatment of aesthetic consciousness and the ontological structure of a work of art are full of rich possibilities. There are many insights in *Truth and Method* that Gadamer calls on in his later essays. The importance of art in relation to philosophy is an on-going concern for Gadamer. He also stresses the importance of an analysis of historical consciousness. This analysis develops more fully the position that he has begun to articulate in the analysis of the experience of art.

23

4

The Experience of History

Gadamer's analysis of aesthetic consciousness is a beginning point for enabling humans to address the issue of alienation. In comparing the experience of art to the concept of aesthetic consciousness that dominates twentieth-century thinking, a fuller concept emerges. This new, or rehabilitated, concept addresses the problem of distance, especially epistemological distance. An epistemological distance is established in the process of knowing when the subject is understood to be separated from, or at a distance from, an object to be known. Gadamer shows us that in the experience of art, humans are not subjects at a distance from the art experienced as object. The analysis of the experience of art shows us the inadequacy of a dualistic self-understanding that places people at an epistemological distance from the world in which they live.

Gadamer's analysis of historical consciousness advances this claim. He makes use of the same dialectical method that he uses in the examination of art. He focuses on the emphasis that the currently held concept places on objective distance. He examines the concept in relationship to lived experience and to pre-Enlightenment concepts. In this examination he shows that there is more in the contemporary concept than we recognize. He brings out what is hidden or covered over in that concept, particularly what is hidden because of the emphasis on objectivity. He develops a rehabilitated concept that enables us to recognize more fully the nature of human understanding as belonging to a world. Understanding always occurs within the

24

community to which we belong.

Gadamer selects a particular concept, play, to facilitate the analysis of aesthetic consciousness. He follows this same process in the analysis of historical consciousness. Several concepts are particularly important for Gadamer. Prejudice, interpretive distance, effective-history, application, and questions are all defining concepts for his work. Gadamer's analysis of each of these concepts develops his critique of historical consciousness.

Historical Consciousness

The consideration of the contemporaneity of art leads Gadamer to examine historical consciousness. Historical consciousness, like aesthetic consciousness, is characterized by distance. Historical consciousness views the historical event, including a work of art, as other. It is objectified. The task of historical consciousness is to reconstruct the world of the historical object in order to grasp its meaning. Gadamer says that this is the task that Schleiermacher set for hermeneutics. Historical consciousness tries to identify the origin and genesis of the event or work. This consciousness attempts to re-establish the thing within the context of its original time. It works to restore the original circumstances in order to grasp meaning.

Gadamer maintains that, while such activities have a certain importance, they cannot really provide the meaning of the event or work. Because humans are historical beings, we can never return to that original time. Indeed, Gadamer suggests that if this is the only approach that is used, then we hand on dead meaning. He suggests that when a work of art is returned from a museum to its original place or when a building is restored to its original condition, these become tourist attractions. They are not really placed in their original circumstances.

Calling on Hegel's thought, Gadamer says that our historical nature really shows us that we must integrate the past, events and works of art, into our world. Gadamer says, "The essential nature of the historical spirit consists not in the restoration of the past but in *thoughtful mediation with contemporary life*" (TM 168-69). Buildings that have been preserved, but remodeled might serve as an example of this sort of thoughtful mediation. The past is there in the building, but as part of contemporary everyday life. In developing the hermeneutical implications of his critique of historical consciousness, Gadamer dwells

25

on a number of important concepts.

Prejudice (*Vorurteil*)

Gadamer acknowledges that the concept of prejudice holds totally negative connotations in both English and German. Yet, he selects this concept as a place to make a beginning for a critique of historical consciousness. The concept of prejudice enables Gadamer to compare historical consciousness to the experience of historical knowledge and so to harmonize the two. Gadamer is rehabilitating the concept of prejudice in order to demonstrate more clearly the way in which human understanding integrally belongs to the world of human experience.

Heidegger's Fore-Structure of Understanding

Gadamer begins his account of prejudice with the presupposition that Heidegger's analysis of human understanding in *Being and Time* is correct. The subtlety and complexity of Gadamer's thought is evident in this move. Before examining the concept of prejudice, he clearly indicates that his examination begins in a framework that he accepts as a "completely correct phenomenological description" (TM 269). He is beginning his analysis with a clearly accepted pre-judgment, a prejudice.

Gadamer accepts what Heidegger calls the fore-structure of understanding. Heidegger's description of the structure of human understanding shows that every interpretation is grounded in a fore-having. In order to understand something, we must already have the thing in advance. We cannot thematically understand something that is not part of the totality of our world. In addition, every interpretation involves fore-sight. Understanding takes a viewpoint on what is had in advance. Heidegger describes this as a first cut for understanding. In addition, every interpretation involves a fore-conception. In every understanding, there is already a decision about how to conceive the thing. We begin with a conceptual framework.

This concept of fore-structure appears complex and is more easily understood with an example. In order to choose to learn something, it already must be part of our lived experience. When a person feels ill and goes to a physician, the illness is already part of that person's world. The person has the illness. This as analogous to fore-having. In diagnosing the illness, the physician applies a viewpoint. In Western society that viewpoint includes the approach of western medicine. The person who is ill also adopts that viewpoint in the selection of a physician. This is analogous to fore-sight. The physician further limits the context in which the disease will be understood by means of the classification of diseases that contemporary medicine uses. Again, the patient will also make use of this classification, perhaps even turning to printed and electronic resources using the classification as a ways to search for information. This is analogous to fore-conception.

Gadamer emphasizes that the recognition that understanding has this fore-structure does not mean that understanding can be capricious. We ought not arbitrarily begin with a particular preconception of something, nor should we allow our preconceptions to go unexamined. Hidden prejudices can, for example, make "us deaf to what speaks to us in tradition" (TM 270). It is important to be aware of bias. Pre-understanding needs to be made conscious and critiqued in order to develop right understanding. However, all understanding involves pre-judgment, prejudice. This includes historical consciousness which claims to completely exclude prejudice and so be objective.

Enlightenment Prejudice Against Prejudice

Gadamer proposes to show that the Enlightenment demand that all prejudice be overcome is a prejudice. He believes that bringing this prejudice to consciousness will enable us to gain a more appropriate understanding of human finitude and its true historical nature.

The Enlightenment understood prejudice as an unfounded judgment. Prejudices are judgments that are not based on fact and that are not grounded in reason, the ultimate source of authority. The Enlightenment attack on prejudice is primarily aimed at Christianity and at claims about Biblical and dogmatic authority. The Enlightenment thinkers maintained that the Bible, like any other historical document, could only claim credibility based on reason. Gadamer writes,

> *What is written down is not necessarily true. We can know better: this is the maxim with which the modern Enlightenment approaches tradition and which ultimately leads it to undertake historical research.* (TM 272)

Gadamer maintains that this approach has dominated the historical sciences since the nineteenth century. Even Romanticism ultimately is based on this position of the Enlightenment.

Romanticism at first seems to be a rejection of the Enlightenment. It glorifies past times, mythology, and the unconscious. But Gadamer shows that Romanticism is actually a mirror image of the Enlightenment. Where the Enlightenment emphasizes a perfection of rational knowledge, Romanticism focuses on a perfect mythical collective consciousness that is prior to all human thought. Both Romanticism and the Enlightenment are based on a break with tradition. Both hold that tradition can only be understood historically, by looking at it as the past did. Both approaches require that understanding must overcome all prejudices.

Just as Gadamer argued that play shows us that we belong to the work of art, he also uses prejudice to show that we belong to history. He writes,

> *Long before we understand ourselves through the process of self-examination, we understand ourselves in a self-evident way in the family, society, and state in which we live....The self-awareness of the individual is only a flickering in the closed circuits of historical life.* (TM 276)

The Enlightenment rejection of pre-judgment, of prejudice, is itself an unexamined prejudice. It leads the Enlightenment and historical consciousness that develops out of the Enlightenment to be blind to the realization that prejudices, far more than individual judgments, constitute the historical reality of human existence. When this is understood, it becomes clear that prejudices are really conditions of human understanding. Without prejudices there is no understanding.

Rehabilitation of the Concept of Prejudice

Gadamer's analysis of prejudice leads him to emphasize the importance of a rehabilitation of the concept of prejudice. He notes that the Enlightenment divided prejudice into those that arise from over-hastiness and those that arise from reliance on authority. In each case, it is assumed that prejudices are false and so prevent humans from coming to correct knowledge. He points out that this approach overlooks, or excludes, the possibility that prejudices can be true.

Gadamer uses the example of authority to illustrate his point about prejudice. People can be misled if they rely on authority, but that is not always the case. Authority can be based in knowledge. He maintains that teachers have authority based on the knowledge that they have. For students to accept the truth of what a teacher says as a starting point for understanding does not serve to mislead students. Rather, beginning with the judgment that what the teacher teaches is correct enables the student to learn and come to fuller knowledge. Moral knowledge is similar. Children often do well to trust the authority of parents concerning how to behave in certain circumstances. To take the moral values of the parent as true may serve a child very well, especially when those values are good values.

Gadamer reinforces the example of authority by means of an examination of tradition. He notes that the Enlightenment treated tradition within its critique of authority. It held tradition to be suspect because it was viewed as a power over against the individual rational consciousness. Tradition encourages individuals to hold dogmatically to pre-given positions, rather than critically examine hypotheses.

Gadamer maintains that tradition is really a part of humans. It is not something that can stand over against people and so be alien or other. People stand within their traditions. The past is present in these traditions. Humans are addressed by their traditions. Religious traditions are particularly illustrative of Gadamer's claim. When a religious community gathers to celebrate a marriage, they engage in a living tradition. Those who marry and those who witness the marriage are all part of a long tradition. In carrying out the marriage ceremony, they transmit the tradition. This can be done in an uncritical manner. But the tradition can be maintained and critiqued at the same time. For example, the tradition may contain elements that encourage the domination of women by men. These destructive prejudices can be critiqued without abandoning the tradition. The tradition can be communicated and preserved without handing on these aspects of the tradition. Yet, the tradition motivates the couple to commit to a life together. That they choose marriage as a way of life is fundamentally constituted by the tradition in which they find themselves.

The critique of tradition as it is handed over reveals the activity of historical consciousness. This consciousness recognizes that it is part of a living tradition and so is formed by that tradition. It also recognizes that it forms the tradition as it hands it over. This is not an arbitrary act of subjectivity. It is not an act of a fully autonomous individual. Rather, it is a fusion of past and present. Gadamer writes,

29

The self-criticism of historical consciousness leads finally to recognizing historical consciousness not only in events but also in understanding itself. <u>Understanding is to be thought of less as a subjective act than as participating in an event of tradition,</u> a process of transmission in which past and present are constantly mediated. (TM 290)

Tradition illustrates that prejudice, pre-understanding, is a condition of the possibility of any understanding. We must already belong to a community of those who understand in order to begin to understand. This does not mean that understanding cannot be critical, but it does require that understanding recognize its situation.

Interpretive Distance

The rehabilitation of the concept of prejudice enables Gadamer to show that the distance that characterizes historical consciousness is not a gulf that inhibits understanding. Historical consciousness is supported by the tradition of which it is a part. In *Truth and Method*, Gadamer calls this distance that is part of the situation of historical consciousness, temporal distance (*Zeitenabstandes*). Heidegger's influence and emphasis on time guide Gadamer in his selection of terminology. When he reflects on *Truth and Method* years later, he notes that other types of distance besides time serve the same function as temporal distance. All of these types of distancing he calls interpretive distance.

Interpretive distance characterizes the human situation of experiencing understanding as a polarity. Humans experience tradition as something with which they are familiar. Tradition is a fundamental, even decisive part, of who we are as humans. Yet, tradition is also strange or alien. Gadamer writes,

Hermeneutics must start from the position that a person seeking to understand something has a bond to the subject matter that comes into language through the tradition from which the text speaks. On the other hand, hermeneutical consciousness is aware that its bond to this subject matter does not consist in some self-evident, unquestioned unanimity, as is the case with the unbroken stream of tradition. (TM 295)

30

Understanding is this play between familiarity and strangeness.

The familiarity that humans experience may include both productive and problematic prejudices. It is impossible to distinguish in advance the productive prejudices that facilitate understanding from the problematic prejudices that result in misunderstanding. Yet, Gadamer notes, in the process of understanding this separation does occur. Humans are able to come to recognize the problematic prejudices and so understand the subject matter that is received in tradition in a different, perhaps better, way.

Interpretive distance facilitates this filtering of prejudices. Gadamer says that interpretive distance, especially in the form of temporal distance, should not be approached as an abyss but as a continuity that enables the past to be present. In any situation of understanding, a certain sort of distancing enables us to see the meaning of the situation or subject matter to be understood.

The simple exercise of writing a paper exemplifies Gadamer's point. When a person writes a first draft of a paper, often unnoticed prejudices are contained in the paper. These prejudices can be as simple as tendencies to use specific expressions in a repetitive manner. Such tendencies have been handed over to the individual in the process of learning to write. Other, more complex prejudices, can enter the writing including assumptions about what it is to be human. If what is written can be set aside for a period of time, the author can return to the paper and recognize some of the prejudices that may inhibit a reader's understanding. As the paper is rewritten, the meaning becomes clearer. However, as anyone who has ever done much writing knows, the process is never completed. One can return to something that has been written many times and still find things to change and issues that need to be addressed. Once something is written and given over to readers, the process of understanding continues. Each reading is a new reading,

Gadamer recognizes that various types of interpretive distance are fundamental to human understanding. For example, this distance can also occur in an encounter with someone who speaks a different language. The attempt to communicate can show us preconceptions in our own language. Gadamer maintains that temporal distance does offer humans special critical help in making evaluations. He notes that this is particularly the case in evaluating art, where temporal distance is often vital for determining the importance of a work.

The recognition of the importance of interpretive distance, and especially of temporal distance, not only challenges people to struggle to identify and correct prejudices that lead to misunderstanding, it also shows us that history has an efficacy within understanding. *"Understanding is, essentially, a historically effected event"* (TM 300).

Effective-History (*Wirkungsgeschichte*)

Effective-history is one of the defining concepts of Gadamer's philosophical hermeneutics. Effective-history is the history in which we all exist. This concept emphasizes that consciousness is not a subject removed from history as an object. Rather consciousness is historically effected consciousness. Gadamer says that we are more being than consciousness. In saying this, he is emphasizing that history places limitations on human consciousness such that we can never go completely beyond these limitations. The analysis of historical consciousness with which Gadamer began results in the recognition of a theoretical requirement that understanding become aware of effective-history.

Recognition of effective-history means that we must become aware of what Gadamer calls the hermeneutical situation. Humans are finite. We always stand within a situation. We cannot stand outside of the situation of our existence and see it from an objective distance where the whole of our existence can be illuminated. Rather, we "light up" our situation from within that situation. Gadamer writes,

> *The illumination of this situation - reflection on effective history - can never be completely achieved; yet the fact that it cannot be completed is due not to a deficiency in reflection but to the essence of the historical being that we are. <u>To be historically means that knowledge of oneself can never be complete</u>.* (TM 302)

Gadamer develops the concepts of horizon and of fusion as part of his reflection on effective-history.

Horizon

In common conversation "horizon" designates everything that can be seen from a particular position. We talk about expanding our horizons and about new horizons. In each case the usage indicates that while we cannot escape being situated, we can move about in the situation and so change our horizon. Both Friedrich Nietzsche and Edmund Husserl use the term "horizon" as a philosophical term. Philosophically, the term has the same implications as in common usage and also emphasizes the ability to move beyond what is nearest and include a greater expanse in the range of understanding. In making this move, one is able to have a better sense of significance. When horizons are very limited, people value what is close but miss the value of things at a distance.

Gadamer notes that historical consciousness has always recognized the need to step into the horizon of another when trying to understand something. When we try to understand another person's position on an issue, we say that we try to understand the standpoint or point of view of that person. We try to stand within that person's horizon. Historical consciousness takes this approach in order to understand something from the past. It does not claim to agree with the position that it takes. It takes the position in order to understand.

Gadamer recognizes that the move that historical consciousness makes is important for understanding. Yet, he says that this description of what happens is incomplete and results in the creation of the sort of historical gap that historical consciousness then takes to be a problem. When we approach understanding as the need to stand in another person's position, what we also do is protect our own position from any challenge. In doing this, we withhold from the other's position the possibility of being true. That is, we prevent it from addressing us and making a claim on us. Historical consciousness claims that there are two horizons. The historian, or the person doing the historical inquiry, claims to be able to move back and forth between the two horizons. The historical document or situation can remain only in its historical horizon.

Gadamer follows the approach that he took in the examination of aesthetic consciousness and again in the examination of prejudice. He asks if historical consciousness is really being accurate when it describes what happens in the process of moving horizons. Gadamer claims that the experience of historical consciousness is not the experience of passing from a familiar world into another, alien, world. He writes,

> *When our historical consciousness transposes itself into historical horizons, this does not entail passing into alien worlds unconnected in any way with our own; instead, they together constitute the one great horizon that moves from within and that, beyond the frontiers of the present, embraces the historical depths*

of our self-consciousness. Everything contained in historical consciousness is in fact embraced by a single historical horizon. (TM 304)

When we stand in another person's position, we put ourselves in that position. We take our own immediate horizon with us. We bring our own concerns and questions to that which we try to understand.

Fusion of Horizons (Horizontverschmelzung)

Gadamer calls this situation in which the present horizon is being formed in conjunction with the past, a fusion of horizons. He says that this process is one in which old and new grow together. In this growth living meaning develops. While Gadamer describes the situation of historical consciousness as formed within one horizon, he suggests that fusion is still an appropriate concept for explaining the process of human understanding. The concept of fusion acknowledges that consciousness distinguishes itself from that which is experienced as other. Yet, this distinguishing is only part of the process of understanding. There is a continual recombining that is also part of the process of understanding. The two horizons are never completely separated, yet, there is a fusion that takes place. Gadamer says, "To bring about this fusion in a regulated way is the task of...historically effected consciousness" (TM 307). This task is what Gadamer calls the problem of application.

Application

In order to explain the importance of the concept of application, Gadamer reviews the history of the development of hermeneutics. He notes that hermeneutics was once divided into three areas: understanding, interpretation , and application. As understanding and interpretation joined, application was set aside. This was particularly true in literary and historical hermeneutics. In legal and theological hermeneutics, aspects of the task of application were retained. Gadamer notes that in both preaching and legal judgments, there is an application in a particular instance of interpretation. Both religious and legal texts are made valid in the process of interpretation. He writes, "the text, whether law or gospel, if it is to be understood properly – i.e., according to the claim it makes – must be understood at every moment, in every concrete situation, in a new and different way" (TM 309). These forms of hermeneutics preserve something fundamental to all understanding. Understanding is always application.

Gadamer says that application shows us that understanding is a process of service, not domination. In the process of understanding an historical event or text, we do not take possession of that event; we do not dominate and control it. Rather, we allow it to take possession of us. The event or text comes to life in and through us.

Gadamer uses legal hermeneutics to illustrate the importance of application for the process of understanding. When a judge interprets the law, the needs of the present are fundamentally important. But this does not mean that the judge's interpretation is arbitrary, or the making of totally new law. The judge must recognize the legal significance in the particular case. While the task of the judge is not to make law, it is to make law live. The judge helps the law speak to the citizens. Moreover, the judge is not exempt from the law. The authority of the law is not an arbitrary authority that is not subject to the law. Rather, the law has authority because it binds everyone, even the judge. The judge is not removed from the implications of the law, but stands within the influence and effects of the law. The judge belongs to the legal situation in which his or her judgment has effects. But the judge does not know the law and then simply place it on a particular case. In considering each case, the judge understands, and interprets for the citizens, the meaning of the law. The judge must remain open to the claim that the law makes. Not every interpretation is allowed within the meaning of the law.

Gadamer maintains that all understanding is like legal understanding. In a sense, each person functions like a judge. We do not first know something and apply that universal knowledge to a particular case. We come to understand the universal through the particular situations and instances of understanding. Effective-historical consciousness recognizes that the task of understanding includes application. This application requires that consciousness be open to the experience of tradition and to the claim to truth encountered in tradition.

Questions and Openness

Gadamer emphasizes that the experience of effective-history shows that openness is fundamental to human understanding. He believes that we best understand this openness which is part of human understanding when we look at the structure of questions. He maintains that the horizon of the question is openness. In other words, in asking a question, we are situated within an open context where we allow ourselves to be addressed by and influenced by something other. We recognize the expanding horizon of our situation. Understanding is a never-ending process. An exploration of the question provides a clearer sense of this openness.

Gadamer distinguishes between rhetorical and legitimate questions. He characterizes legitimate questions as opening up what is asked after. Learning experiences serve to illustrate both types of questions. A teacher can ask rhetorical questions. These are questions that require the students to tell the teacher what he or she wants to hear. These sorts of questions inhibit and even end discussions. But a teacher can ask legitimate questions. These questions are aimed at opening the conversation. No correct answer is presupposed. A teacher who asks legitimate questions helps students to delve more deeply into the course materials and the meaning of those materials.

Gadamer notes that questions establish horizons for understanding. Every question brings with it the prejudices, the presuppositions, of the questioner. Questions can, therefore, be right or wrong. When someone asks a wrong question, that question serves to distort the matter under discussion. What happens is that the horizon is moved by the question. The horizon in which the matter of discussion is considered is dominated by an opinion rather than being opened to discussion. An appropriate question opens the subject matter so that a conversation can emerge. A teacher who raises a good question opens the classroom to the exploration of the matter under discussion. Gadamer says that the person who knows how to ask questions preserves an orientation towards openness. "The art of questioning is the art of questioning ever further – i.e., the art of thinking" (TM 367).

This art of thinking acknowledges that to ask a question requires a person to admit ignorance. It also requires that a person want to know. Gadamer says that questioning is "more a passion than an action" (TM 366). Questions present themselves to those who want to understand. Moreover, the person who develops the art of questioning searches for everything that supports a position. This is not the art of argumentation that tries to destroy positions. Rather, questioning develops thinking by bringing out the strength of a position. This also prevents the suppression by the dominant position of other positions.

Legitimate questions and the art of asking these questions show us that understanding requires a context of openness. This openness enables the thinker to meet something that addresses him or her and to respond to that address. Openness results in a dialogue.

Summary of Gadamer's Critique of Historical Consciousness

Gadamer's rehabilitation of the concept of prejudice and his analysis of the concepts of interpretive distance, effective-history, application, and questions constitute a rehabilitation of the concept of historical consciousness. Historical consciousness as developed through the Enlightenment is like aesthetic consciousness. It believes that it is at an epistemological distance from what it tries to understand. This consciousness projects an abyss between the subject that is trying to understand and the object that is the focus of understanding.

Gadamer's rehabilitation of the concept of prejudice begins his critique of this conceptualization of historical consciousness. His work on the concept of prejudice leads to the recognition that understanding always presupposes a certain judgment about that which is understood. Understanding cannot be objective in the sense of being free of presuppositions. Indeed, without belonging to a community of those who understand and without participating in the traditions, and so the prejudices of that community, there is no possibility of human understanding.

However, Gadamer recognizes that understanding is not simply the handing over of the past with all of its prejudices unchanged and unchallenged. Human understanding develops interpretive distance and so is able to filter prejudices, distinguishing productive and problematic prejudices.

Interpretive distance shows humans that history is effective in understanding. History places limitations on understanding. These limitations are, however, fluid. They constitute the horizon of understanding. Yet, thinkers can move within the situations in which they find themselves and so shift their horizons. This shifting enables consciousness to distinguish itself from and identify itself with history.

Gadamer uses the concept of application to illustrate this movement.

Gadamer develops the concept of application to show that understanding is not an act of domination of an object by a subject. Rather, understanding is the process of serving meaning. In order to do this, understanding must remain open. The task of understanding is the task of learning to ask appropriate questions. In the process of asking questions, historical consciousness is able to understand that it is hermeneutical consciousness. It does not stand in alienation from its past. Rather, it is in constant conversation with that past in the course of living in the present.

By means of this rehabilitation of historical consciousness, Gadamer points to the importance of conversation and so of language for the possibility of any understanding.

5

The Experience of Language

In *Truth and Method*, Gadamer develops philosophical hermeneutics, emphasizing that all understanding is self-understanding. Through the rehabilitation of the concept of aesthetic consciousness, he begins to develop a philosophical position that overcomes the sense of alienation that results from Enlightenment thinking, especially from the distinction of subject from object. He examines the experience of art, moving to the insight that we belong to our world in an integral manner.

In rehabilitating the concept of historical consciousness, he further develops this experience of belonging. It becomes evident that understanding is a process in which each finite human participates. We enter a particular point in that process and so are affected by what has gone before us. We have certain prejudices because we are part of this process. These prejudices form and make possible our understandings. Yet, as finite humans, we can still develop interpretive distance and so filter prejudices. We cannot remove ourselves from the situation to which we belong, but we can move around within that situation and so change our horizons. In this process we experience the fusion of horizons. We are not beings alienated and isolated from the past. Rather, we are a living part of an ongoing conversation. We are active participants in a dialogue with the past that will carry on into the future.

This dialogue is mediated through the medium of language.

The third part of *Truth and Method* turns to an examination of language. Gadamer writes, "The guiding idea of the following discussion is *that the fusion of horizons that takes place in understanding is actually the achievement of language*" (TM 378). He begins the discussion of language with a quotation from Schleiermacher, "Everything presupposed in hermeneutics is but language." In the process of his own analysis of language he writes, "*Being that can be understood is language*" (TM 474). The examination of language is, therefore, central and fundamental to Gadamer's philosophical position. It retains this position in his thinking for the rest of his career.

In the third part of *Truth and Method*, Gadamer examines language as what he calls the medium of human experience. This examination is a further development of the fusion that he first notes in aesthetic consciousness and develops more fully in the analysis of historical consciousness. He traces the history of the emergence of the concept of language in order to demonstrate that he is not imposing something on language. This follows his approach in the first two parts of *Truth and Method*. He emphasizes that the concept of language as he sets it out is part of the process of the historical emergence of a concept of language. Finally, he sets out a concept of language as the horizon of a hermeneutic ontology. We are situated within language and in that situation we understand everything that is, including ourselves.

Language as a Medium

Gadamer makes the claim that, "All understanding is interpretation, and all interpretation takes place in the medium of a language that allows the object to come into words and yet is at the same time the interpreter's own language" (TM 389). It is important to recognize that, in making this claim that language is a medium, Gadamer is rejecting the concept that language is a tool that can be used by a subject to achieve control over or to manipulate an object. Language serves the object in that it lets it come into meaning. In like manner, understanding as it takes place in language is not a means for domination. Understanding is a process of coming to agreement. Moreover, if all understanding takes place in language, then humans must be situated within language in order to understand.

Gadamer uses the example of translation to illustrate his claim.

40

When a person learns a new language, the initial process is often that of moving back and forth between a language that is understood and the language that one is learning. For example, in this book a number of German words have been introduced. If you do not know German, you may not immediately understand *Spiel*. You may even have paused at this point in your reading to leaf back through the pages to discover how to translate the word (play). Once you have the word in English, you understand what is meant and can go on reading this passage and understand further. If you did not understand the word and no translation into English was immediately available, you might try to figure out the meaning of the word from the rest of the context. Notice, that what you are trying to do is to translate the word into a language that is your own, a language that you speak and understand. What you want is to understand the meaning.

A translator of a text carries out a similar exercise. This person is comfortable in both languages and conducts a conversation that makes what is spoken in one language intelligible in another language. While this can be done in a dictionary fashion replacing each word in one language with a word in the other language, such translations are usually weak. In a good translation, the translator is involved in the subject under discussion and so finds the best way to make that subject intelligible in the second language. This may require a translation that is far from literal. The appropriate language is recognized because understanding takes place.

Conversing with someone who speaks a different language provides yet a further illustration of Gadamer's point. The traveler in Florence who wants to go to Rome by train arrives at the train station and does not know which track is the correct track. Time is of the essence. If the traveler can identify someone who is willing to try to arrive at a common understanding, despite the different languages, then the traveler will make it to Rome. Translation will have to occur and one or the other of the two people will have to suddenly understand.

Each of these examples illustrates Gadamer's claim that language is not a tool. In each case, finding a common language "coincides with the very act of understanding and reaching agreement" (TM 388). Language is a medium. Just as the air we breathe is a medium in which we live, so we live within language. Just as we can overlook the importance of the air to us because it is so close to us, so also we can overlook language and the sustaining role it plays for all human understanding. Gadamer suggests that these examples show the intimacy of speaking and thinking.

41

The Object of Understanding

Gadamer uses what he terms the "hermeneutic phenomenon" to illustrate the structure of this intimacy between language and understanding. He writes,

> *The essential relation between language and understanding is seen primarily in the fact that the essence of tradition is to exist in the medium of language, so that the preferred <u>object</u> of interpretation is a verbal one.* (TM 389)

He notes that linguistic tradition, texts of various sorts, are not simply remnants of the past. They are intended to be handed down and so are tradition in the truest sense. Gadamer is calling on the German word *Überlieferung*, which translates as "tradition" when he makes this comment. Literally, *Überlieferung* is a handing over. A written text is a gift that is given from one person and from one period to another.

Gadamer's point is that in the written text we have a paradigmatic example of the object of understanding. That object has its being in language. It is not bound to the mind of the author, to the original audience, or to the contemporary reader. We might say that it has a life of its own, but a life that is within the horizon of language. In an essay written in 1960, the same year in which *Truth and Method* was published, Gadamer says that our experience of the relationship of words and things suggests that it is appropriate to say that "things bring themselves to expression in language" (PH 81).

The Process of Understanding

Gadamer maintains that hermeneutics not only demonstrates that the object of understanding has its being within language, it also shows us that the process of understanding is fundamentally linguistic. Gadamer says,

> *When we are concerned with understanding and interpreting verbal texts, interpretation in the medium of language itself shows what understanding always is: assimilating what is said to the point that it becomes one's own.* (TM 398)

42

Gadamer maintains that the process of interpretation, and so the process of understanding, is not an attempt to draw attention to oneself. Rather, it is a movement of openness, of meeting the object of understanding. The text that is handed over in the tradition has its life in language. The task of interpretation, which is the process of understanding, is to find the right language to understand the text. If the tradition is to live, it must be appropriated. Each new generation and each person must be able to make the tradition their own. Gadamer holds that this appropriation takes place in language. The process of understanding is not one in which a subject can impose any meaning on a text. Because the text has a life in language, it is both open to interpretation and binds the interpreter to finding a right interpretation. This process is much like the process of translation. For example, when the people at the train station in Florence understood each other, language became less visible. While they struggled to understand each other, they focused on language. As soon as they arrived at a right interpretation, language disappeared. Gadamer is not suggesting that we are bound to tradition in a way that does not allow critique and change. Clearly the concept of application that he developed in the examination of historical consciousness makes it clear that understanding is ongoing and that there are many right interpretations of a text. He is emphasizing, that when we understand, we enter into language and are bound by the horizon of language. Just as the object of understanding has its life within language, so also the subject who understands is situated within language.

In discussing the process of understanding, Gadamer is aware of the variety of nonverbal human expressions. He writes,

> *Verbal interpretation is the form of all interpretation, even when what is to be interpreted is not linguistic in nature - i. e., is not a text but a statue or a musical composition. We must not let ourselves be confused by forms of interpretation that are not verbal but in fact presuppose language.* (TM 398)

Each of these types of expression can be understood. The process of understanding is a process of interpretation in which the work is brought to life. The interpretation is not a re-creating of the original work. The performance of a musical work is not the creation of a new work. But the performance brings the work to life. Gadamer says that the reproduction of the musical work "makes is appear as itself for the first time" (TM 399). Moreover, every performance can be presented in words, even if that is not the preferred medium of the performer.

Gadamer is not reducing all understanding to spoken language. He is showing that interpretation and understanding are bound together and that all understanding has the possibility of a verbal interpretation. He recognizes that language sometimes seems inadequate to the task of understanding. We have all had the experience of a work of art or of an experience of nature where we are left speechless. We may have tried to describe symptoms of illness to a physician and not had language for the inner sensations. Yet, Gadamer points out that these limitations are with the particular language conventions that we use. The examples actually confirm the close connection between understanding and language. They point to the conceptual character of all understanding. We search for concepts that will provide intelligibility for our experiences. Moreover, these examples indicate the capacity of any language to continually develop concepts.

Gadamer's philosophy is difficult for the contemporary thinker to follow at this point. For the most part, we presuppose that language is a tool. Gadamer wants to show us that language is the medium in which we exist. In a short essay written in 1966, he says,

> *Hence, language is the real medium of human being, if we only see it in the realm that it alone fills out, the realm of human being-together, the realm of common understanding, and ever-replenished common agreement - a realm as indispensable to human life as the air we breathe.* (PH 68)

Gadamer wants us to experience language as this medium. In so doing, he believes that we will recognize that there is a close connection between understanding and language. Neither can be experienced simply as an object. If we can develop a more appropriate concept of language, we will also develop a better self-understanding. Gadamer again carries out a process of concept rehabilitation. If Gadamer is correct, the rehabilitation of the concept of language has tremendous implications for our understanding of what it is to be human.

History of the Concept of Language

Gadamer again uses the approach that he used in the analysis of aesthetic and historical consciousness. He looks at the history of the concept to find aspects of the experience of language that will show that other eras have experienced language as a medium and that these

44

experiences can help us rehabilitate the concept. Gadamer's many years of teaching Greek philosophy in order to survive the Nazi era, lead him to turn to Greek philosophy. He notes that the Greeks did not have a word for language. Word and object were taken to be intimately united, such that a person's name is part of that person's being. With the development of Greek philosophy, this presupposed unity is called into question. Plato's *Cratylus* explores this problem. Gadamer summarizes the discussions in this dialogue and comes to the conclusion that Plato's work really sets the direction for the modern instrumentalist view of language. Rather than giving Gadamer a basis for claiming that language is most appropriately experienced as a medium, Greek conceptual thought seems to support the claim that language is a tool.

Gadamer reviews this early philosophical beginning, pointing out some of the problems with its formulation. He particularly notes that limiting the possibilities for understanding language to the sort of being that belongs to an image or the sort of being that belongs to a sign prevented Greek thought from considering that language could have its own mode of being, different from either of these. Gadamer, therefore, views the Greek beginnings as moving humans away from an experience of the nature of language. He asserts,

> *Experience is not wordless to begin with, subsequently becoming an object of reflection by being named, by being subsumed under the universality of the word. Rather, experience of itself seeks and finds words that express it. We seek the right word - i.e., the word that really belongs to the thing - so that in it the thing comes into language. Even if we keep in mind that this does not imply any simple copying, the word still belongs to the thing insofar as a word is not a sign coordinated to the thing ex post facto.* (TM 417)

Gadamer turns from Greek thought to the Christian idea of Incarnation, claiming that this concept enables Western thought to retain a sense of the nature of language.

In Christian theology, the Incarnation is the event of the Word becoming flesh. It is the concept that Jesus, while fully human was also fully God. Gadamer makes use of Christian Trinitarian thought, especially as found in the Gospel of John. This thought emphasizes that Jesus is the Word. This theology holds that the Word was there at creation and will be eternally with God. Not only does the Word become flesh in the Incarnation, it remains Word. Gadamer makes use

45

of the theological reflection on the Word to show that in medieval scholastic thought there are two insights into the nature of language that were not part of Greek thought.

First, Gadamer finds in this theology the realization that words are not the mind seeking to express itself, but rather seeking to express the object. He notes that Thomas Aquinas suggests that the word is like light in that it makes color visible. Secondly, he says that we can learn from scholastic thought that language has an event character. Protestant theology, in particular, emphasizes that the meaning of Christ and the resurrection cannot be separated from the proclamation of the event. Meaning and proclamation constitute a unity. Yet, there are multiple proclamations. This insight is similar to the structure of celebration that Gadamer noticed in aesthetic experience. The same event comes to life in many celebrations. The same word is proclaimed in many proclamations. It is also connected to the concept of application that he developed in the analysis of historical consciousness. The meaning of the event is open-ended and on-going.

It might seem, at this point in the development of Gadamer's philosophical position, that he could be charged with using his own presuppositions in an unreflective manner. Clearly he is calling on Western and Christian concepts. The work that these concepts do for Gadamer is very important for the overall development of his claims about the nature of language. He recognizes a mode of being in the concept of Incarnation that he then uses to understand the nature of language. However, other religious traditions do offer support for Gadamer's claims, even though he does not make use of the concepts of these traditions. For example, in Buddhism there is a concept of Chenrezi. This is a fully enlightened Buddha who takes the form of a Bodhisattva, one who remains with the suffering to benefit all beings. Chenrezi is the source of all Buddhas and Bodhisatvas as well as the embodiment of compassion. So, it is correct to say that Chenrezi is the unity of all Buddhas and that Chenrezi is each manifestation. This concept has the event structure that Gadamer finds in the Christian concept of Incarnation.

The insight that Gadamer develops out of the concept of the Incarnation is that when language is seen as having the character of an event rather than of an image or a sign, the process of concept formation can be understood in a more appropriate and philosophically significant way. He suggests that some Christian thought understands language from the context of its event character. He particularly believes that the work of Nicholas of Cusa (1401-1464) develops in this direction. Nicholas held that God is ineffable. God cannot be known by human minds. Moreover, there are identities in God that for humans can only be grasped in distinctions. Gadamer reads Nicholas as recognizing that humans in their speaking cannot achieve a grasp of the order of things as they would appear to an infinite mind, to God. Language must be understood in the context of human finitude. But this finitude does not exclude the possibility of a relationship to divine infinitude. So also, while there are many languages, universal concepts are formed. Yet, finite humans possess the whole of thought only in temporal succession. Gadamer reflects his own position as well as that of Nicholas when he writes,

> But that means...that the general concept meant by the word is enriched by any given perception of a thing, so that what emerges is a new, more specific word formation which does more justice to the particularity of that act of perception. However certainly speaking implies using pre-established words with general meanings, at the same time, a constant process of concept formation is going on, by means of which the life of language develops. (TM 429)

Gadamer sees in language the same structure of finitude that characterizes human existence. A more considered account of language will also facilitate a fuller account of what it is to be human.

Language as Horizon

The final portion of *Truth and Method* develops Gadamer's fundamental position. He maintains that the human world, the world of our lived experience, is linguistic. The concept of horizon that he developed in conjunction with the analysis of historic consciousness is important. Language forms the horizon of human experience. It provides the parameters in which all experience takes place, but it is also a space that can expand and contract and in which humans are situated and can move.

47

Linguistic Nature of the Human World

Gadamer calls on further history of thought about language to begin his reflections. He focuses on the achievements of Wilhelm von Humboldt (1767-1835). Humboldt's work showed that each human language is a mirror of a culture. While Humboldt's work is monumental and contains many paths that Gadamer does not pursue, what Gadamer emphasizes from Humboldt's work is that "*a language-view is a worldview*" (TM 442). The human world is not first without language and then emerges into language. Language is not something that humans possess in the world along with other tools or capabilities. The world of human existence is linguistic. Gadamer reflects on Humboldt's insight and writes, "Not only is the world world only insofar as it comes into language, but language, too, has its real being only in the fact that the world is presented in it" (TM 443). Gadamer concludes that humans are primordially linguistic. Human experience is linguistic in a basic or fundamental sense. He illustrates this claim by looking at human freedom from environment, at what he calls factualness (*Sachlichkeit*), and at community.

Gadamer describes the human relationship to the world as characterized by freedom from environment. This means that, unlike other living creatures, humans can rise above their surroundings to experience world. Humans can experience their environment in meaningful relationships. This involves taking a free, distanced, position in relation to world. Gadamer maintains that it is in language that this freedom is attained. Being able to name things is at the same time being able to rise above them and, in a sense, stand apart from them. Language enables the human relationship to the world to be variable. Animals other than humans can understand and communicate, but the human experience of the world is factual.

Factualness is a philosophical concept that may at first be difficult to comprehend. Gadamer is trying to demonstrate that human experience of the world as factual is a result of our experiencing the world linguistically. Something is factual in that it is recognized and taken as significant by humans. Insofar as this happens, the thing can be spoken of and become the subject matter of conversation between humans. The kind of distance involved in factualness is what Gadamer terms interpretive distance in his discussion of historical consciousness. Factualness is achieved, but it is always situational. The stress here is that it is a human world that presents itself.

In explaining the concept of factualness, Gadamer distinguishes it

48

from scientific objectivity. He explains scientific objectivity as seeking to remove all aspects of subjectivity. What is known objectively is taken to be known independently of human needs and desires. At the same time, it seeks to place the knower above the world so that the world is seen as an object. An object can be measured, calculated, manipulated, and controlled. Scientific objectivity makes it possible to dominate objects.

Gadamer's concept of factualness emphasizes that this scientific form of making things into objects is not the primary way that humans exist in the world. This does not mean that the scientific approach is not important for contemporary humanity. But, scientific objectivity is not able to provide the fullest insight into human existence, including our linguistic experience. We cannot rise above this world as science might suggest and see the world as an object. The world that comes into language is the world as it is significant to humans. Human speaking brings things into the world. Gadamer writes,

> *Just as things, those units of our experience of the world that are constituted by their suitability and their significance, are brought into language, so the tradition that had come down to us is again brought to speak in our understanding and interpretation of it. The linguistic nature of this bringing into language is the same as that of the human experience of the world in general.* (TM 456)

Factualness shows us that we do not dominate and control the world of our experience. Human speaking facilitates the development and growth of world by submitting, by enduring, by allowing ourselves to be taken hold of by the thing. In our speaking, things are able to move into language and so become part of the human world.

In addition to freedom and factualness as examples of the basic linguistic character of human experience, Gadamer notes that the basic linguistic nature of humans is evident in human community. He says "language has its true being only in dialogue" (TM 446). It is in language that human world is disclosed. This world is not the space of isolated individuals. Gadamer says the world is common ground. Human communities are linguistic communities. Language, as conversation, is the process of coming to understand, of reaching agreement. Humans live in the language process, entering into a community in which language is communication. In conversation, language is formed and developed.

Gadamer's analysis of the human experience of the world as linguistic is aimed at moving us to the recognition that we live within language. In language we are able to meet the world in a human manner. Things take on factualness, significance for human existence that can be communicated in conversation with others. In community, humans develop language, and so the experience of language also reveals that humans are communal, part of an ongoing conversation. Gadamer's position maintains that language is a medium. It is where the world and humans experience an original belonging together. *Truth and Method* began with the experience of alienation. In part, Gadamer has shown that this alienation is only possible because of a more fundamental experience of belonging. The nature of this belonging requires further consideration. Gadamer is concerned to emphasize that the sort of belonging that is characteristic of human existence, and so characteristic of language, is finite.

Language as a Speculative Medium

Gadamer maintains that "in language the order and structure of our experience itself is originally formed and constantly changed" (TM 457). In language our experience unfolds. Gadamer is concerned to avoid the claim that what happens in language is a progressive development of knowledge, such that we get closer and closer to a totality such as an infinite intellect would contain. We do not overcome our finitude. In order to explain this aspect of his thinking, Gadamer make use of the concept of speculative structure. The term "speculative" refers to following the dialectical movement of thought and is adapted from Hegel. But Gadamer does not completely agree with Hegel's understanding of the movement of speculative thought. Indeed, Gadamer often notes that he seeks to restore what Hegel calls "bad infinity" to a place of honor. For Hegel, this bad infinity is tinged with finitude. It is "bad" or spurious because it is not the real infinite. It is never a complete totality. Gadamer views this as a strength. Bad infinity shows us that we are finite even as we reach out towards infinity. He writes in his autobiographical statement, "totality is never an object but rather a world-horizon which encloses us and within which we live our lives" (Hahn 37).

While Gadamer does not specifically make the claim, it might be said that language is this bad infinity. He writes,

> *Language is the record of finitude not because the structure of human language is multifarious but because every language is*

50

constantly being formed and developed the more it expresses its experience of the world. It is finite not because it is not at once all other languages, but simply because it is language. (TM 457)

Gadamer tries to follow the experience of finitude that is available to us when we recognize that language is the horizon of all experience. He suggests that the structure of language is speculative, and that this means that language remains finite while allowing an infinity of meaning to be represented.

Gadamer's discussion of the speculative structure of language begins with an account of belonging (*Zugehörigkeit*). He is again concerned that the account of the human experience of language not be restricted to experiencing language as something that humans use. If we experience within the horizon of language, then we belong to language.

Playing on the connection of the German words, he looks at the dialectic of hearing (*hören*). He suggests that hearing is unique in that the one addressed must hear, whether or not that person wants to hear. Moreover, hearing is an "avenue to the whole" (TM 462). Gadamer's brief treatment of the dialectic of hearing needs development, but the point that he is trying to make is clear. In hearing, the hearer is reached; and in hearing language, the hearer is reached by a whole, by being which can be understood. It is not human action that brings about hearing. Belonging means that we are addressed. Gadamer maintains that the coming into language of a thing is not our action on the thing, but the act of the thing itself. He does not mean that thinking and human concept development are unimportant. But just as hearing requires humans to listen, thinking requires that we "follow the subject matter itself" (TM 464). The experience of understanding is the experience of having something happen to you; it is a passion. In interpreting a text, the task is to let the text exert itself. Just as hearing is reached by a whole, the words that interpretatively express a text also express the whole of the meaning of the text.

Gadamer selects the concept "speculative" as particularly helpful for describing the experience of the whole that is possible within the finitude of language and so within the finitude of human experience. He writes,

Language itself, however, has something speculative about it ...as the realization of meaning, as the event of speech, of mediation, of coming to an understanding. Such a realization is speculative in that the finite possibilities of the word are oriented toward the

sense intended as toward the infinite. (TM 469)

Language is speculative, not because it reflects individual beings, but because it directs back to the whole of being. Gadamer exemplifies this with the examples of everyday speech and poetic word.

In everyday speech, when someone has something to say to someone else, the words to facilitate understanding must be sought out. Not everything that is meant is said, but what is said opens out towards the unsaid. A daily conversation seems to be a simple activity. Yet, what is present in that conversation is a world. The language we speak is open; particular expressions carry with them the whole horizon of language. Our conversations are ongoing even when they break off. They refer backward and forward. To make his point, Gadamer compares this openness of everyday speech to the statements required in a court of law. Only what is said can be understood as part of the case. In this situation, when meaning is reduced to what is said, distortion is inevitable. The witness who really wants to get at the truth of the situation wants to say more and wants to enter into dialogue. But in the court, meaning is assigned to an event rather than taking it from the event. What is said in everyday language is essentially bound to what it expresses, not in such a way as to determine it totally but recognizing its relation to the whole by not attempting to exclude the unsaid. The poetic word intensifies this relation to the whole of being. Gadamer says that the poetic work opens up a world by giving a new view. Words are allowed to take on new meaning in order to bring about new world. In each case language is speculative because it in it finite experience opens out towards the infinite while remaining finite. In "The Nature of Things and the Language of Things" Gadamer expresses this more clearly. He says that language "exhibits an experience that is always finite but that nowhere encounters a barrier at which something infinite is intended that can barely be surmised and no longer spoken" (PH 80).

The Space of Human Belonging Together

Gadamer's treatment of language culminates his work in philosophical hermeneutics. No summary can do justice to the importance of the step that his philosophy takes in the process of rehabilitating the concept of language. Gadamer's recognition that no interpretation or translation is "as understandable as the original" (PH

68) is important to remember. The task of the interpreter is to try to stand within the general direction of what is interpreted and to carry on that direction in the interpretation. There is much more that could be said about Gadamer's work on language. Three final points about the peculiar character of language that Gadamer emphasizes in the essay "Man and Language" published in 1966, serve to help readers to continue to think in the direction that Gadamer has begun.

The first characteristic that he sets out it the "essential self-forgetfulness that belongs to language" (PH 64). When language is functioning well, human speakers are unaware of language and its structure and grammar. In learning a language, we translate from the new language back into the language we know. The new language and language in general are very visible. The moment that we actually begin to understand in the new language, the language itself disappears. Gadamer says that what is evident in this experience is that the real "being of language consists in what is said in it" (PH 65). Language takes us into a common world that we share with the living and dead.

Language is also characterized by I-lessness. Language is never purely private; it belongs to community. Gadamer's emphasis on the importance of understanding language from out of the experience of human conversation emphasizes this characteristic. Even when we talk to ourselves or carry out an inner dialogue, we speak to someone.

Finally, Gadamer points to what he calls the universality of language. He says that nothing is excluded from language. Language is the realm of the speakable. This is a realm of common understanding and ever-renewing and re-working agreement. In following the directions set by Gadamer, humans are encouraged to think about language as the space in which we belong together. We are not isolated subjects. We are part of a living tradition and community. It is within this horizon that we can come to understand ourselves and the nature of human finitude.

53

6

The Universality of Hermeneutics

Gadamer's work in *Truth and Method* on aesthetic consciousness, historical consciousness, and language supports his position that hermeneutics must be philosophy. He recognizes that hermeneutics began as methodology of interpretation and developed as a methodology for the humanities. In his reflections on his philosophical journey, he explains the conclusion that he draws as the recognition of,

> *The indissoluble connection between thinking and speaking* which compels hermeneutics to become philosophy. *One must always think in a language, even if one does not always have to think in the same language. Hermeneutics cannot evade claiming universality because language as linquisticality - Sprachlichkeit - constitutes a human capacity inseparably linked with rationality as such.* (Hahn 25)

His younger colleague, Jürgen Habermas, challenges Gadamer's claim that the universality of hermeneutics is inescapable. This challenge developed into what is usually referred to as the Habermas-Gadamer debate. In keeping with Gadamer's philosophical hermeneutics, it is appropriate to view the exchange between the two philosophers as a conversation. The conversation begins with Gadamer's claim for the universality of hermeneutics and is continued with Habermas' questions and challenges to Gadamer's thought and Gadamer's further thinking based on Habermas' contributions to the conversation. English speakers who want to read the translated primary texts that constitute this conversation can find most of them anthologized in *The Hermeneutic Tradition*, edited by Galye L. Ormiston and Alan D. Schrift. Unless otherwise noted, page references in this chapter refer to that volume.

Gadamer on the Universality of Hermeneutics

Gadamer's essay, "The Universality of the Hermeneutical Problem," published in 1966, is the most concise explanation of his understanding of what it means to claim universality for hermeneutics. He begins the essay by asking why the problem of language has become so central for twentieth-century philosophical discussions. He suggests that the best way to approach this question is indirectly by addressing the question,

> *Of how our natural view of the world - the experience of the world that we have as we simply live out our lives - is related to the unassailable and anonymous authority that confronts us in the pronouncements of science.* (147)

He maintains that the task of philosophy since the seventeenth century has been this mediation of the totality of human experience with the way in which humans develop their capabilities to know. Philosophy in the twentieth century has turned to language to approach this issue. Gadamer believes that this is appropriate since language is the fundamental way in which we live in the world. The task of philosophy is to bring together the "world of technology" with an experience of things within the world as neither "arbitrary nor manipulable."

In beginning to address this task, Gadamer explains how aesthetic consciousness, historical consciousness, and hermeneutical consciousness all embody forms of alienation. His accounts of aesthetic and historical consciousness have already been treated in Chapters 3 and 4. He repeats what he has already developed in *Truth and Method* emphasizing that when aesthetic consciousness claims sovereignty in the experience of art, there is "an alienation when compared to the authentic experience that confronts us in the form of art" (148). Similarly, historical consciousness "knows only an alienated form of ... historical tradition" (150). Hermeneutical consciousness, when understood as Schleiermacher developed it, is a methodology employed to avoid misunderstanding. It, too, assumes that the task of understanding stands in relationship to something alien. Gadamer maintains that the task of philosophy is to overcome the alienation in all three forms of consciousness.

Continuing to summarize his work in *Truth and Method*, Gadamer maintains that all of these forms of consciousness overlook the manner in which humans already are connected to the work of art or to the past, prior to any attempt to understand art or history. He repeats the claim that he made in his earlier work, "It is not so much our judgments as it is our prejudices that constitute our being" (151). The rehabilitation of the concepts of prejudice and authority shows us that it is because we are possessed by something that we are able to be open to something new. Gadamer says that this is the recognition of the hermeneutical circle, our understanding is always conditioned by a pre-understanding. Without this conditionedness, no understanding is possible.

Gadamer advances his position by maintaining that the problem of alienation presented in the examples of aesthetic and historical consciousness is also a problem of natural science. The methodology developed by natural science serves to distance people from the lived experience of the world. Biological research can serve as an example of Gadamer's point. A research biologist often works in a laboratory, isolating life from its ecological setting. The biologist may not have any knowledge of field biology. The life that the biologist studies is not life as experienced in daily life, but rather life as alienated, or removed, from that situation. Gadamer suggests that alienation is especially brought about by the technological attitude toward the world that is part of modern science. This attitude focuses on domination and control.

Gadamer does not suggest that what is needed is the abandonment of science or the limitation of scientific exploration. Yet, he is concerned that the technological purposes of science can result in a world of destruction. He asks, "If the presuppositions of these possibilities for knowing and making remain half in the dark, cannot the result be that the hand applying this knowledge will be destructive?" (153). Gadamer's position is developed, in part, out of his experience as a German during the period of both the First and Second World Wars. He elaborates his concern with the example of statistics. Statistics are particularly useful for the development of propaganda.

Correct mastery of the methodology involved in statistics does not ensure that the methods will be used for productive human purposes. He notes that while statistics appear to yield objective facts, "which questions these facts answer and which facts would begin to speak if other questions were asked are hermeneutical questions" (153). Gadamer concludes that philosophical hermeneutics is not restricted to the humanities, but includes the natural sciences. Indeed, Gadamer holds that philosophical hermeneutics includes all forms of human understanding. The problem that hermeneutics addresses is universal. The natural sciences also need to ask hermeneutical questions.

Gadamer argues that the development of productive questions is not a result of the application of methodology. Such questions require imagination, the ability to see what is questionable. In science this does not mean the abandonment of method. Rather, scientists need to know their method so well that it is placed within the whole of experience. Within this experience of the whole, fruitful ideas can emerge. This happens not by following the methodology, but by asking how a certain experience fits within the whole. Gadamer refers to Newton's experience with the falling apple as an example. He maintains that what we observe, even in science, is the fundamental linguistic constitution of the world. Science is situated within what Gadamer calls the logic of question and answer. This logic is fundamentally linguistic. The reason which science calls on is not outside of or alien to language, but is constituted within language.

Gadamer further illustrates his point with the example of how a child learns to know his or her mother or learns to speak. While we may point to a particular occurrence of a first word for a child, we cannot really identify when a child learns to speak. For that first word to emerge, there must already be a world interpreted and familiar. The child does not speak out of an experience of strangeness, but rather out of a sense of belonging. The same process is true for knowledge of the mother. Gadamer uses the examples to show that common understanding and familiarity, what he called belongingness in *Truth and Method*, make possible "the venture into the alien" and the "enrichment of our own experience of the world" *(156)*.

Gadamer's point is that the claim to universality of hermeneutics needs to be understood as the claim that all understanding is bound to language. This is the position that he maintained at the end of *Truth and Method*. Humans live within language. Every encounter with reality presupposes linguisticality, the linguistic constitution of understanding. Human reason cannot hold a position outside of language and then translate that position into language. Even reason is constituted linguistically. The hermeneutic task is to elucidate linguistic constitution. This does not mean that we are confined to a system of signs or to linguistic relativism. Any language in which we live opens into "the infinite realm of possible expression" (157). But no type of rationality stands outside of language. Knowledge is always in response to a question. Science is not excluded from this linguistically constituted world, nor does science control the world of our lived experience. Science is part of the dialogue that we are. Gadamer says of this dialogue that it is "the infinite dialogue" that "is opened in the direction of the truth that we are" (157).

Habermas and the Critique of Hermeneutics

Jürgen Habermas engaged Gadamer in conversations about hermeneutics and the claim of philosophical hermeneutics to universality. In 1971 he published "The Hermeneutic Claim to Universality." In this essay, he maintains that science is capable of arriving at truth claims about things monologically. Science can deal with things without the medium of language. Science can form theories that are removed from the world of everyday language. Habermas questions the close relationship between reason and language in Gadamer's work. Moreover, he maintains that the model of reason as independent from the presuppositions of everyday language is fundamental to the development of human knowledge. While Habermas rejects the claim of philosophical hermeneutics to universality, he suggests that the development of philosophical hermeneutics is significant. This sort of philosophical thought does have a role to play in relation to modern science. It can assist in the "translation of important scientific information into the language of the social life-world" (250). However, philosophical hermeneutics is not justified in making the claim to universality.

Habermas uses the example of psychoanalysis to further refute the hermeneutic claim to universality and to correctly position the philosophical use of hermeneutics. He proposes that his discussion defends philosophical hermeneutics and shows how to best understand what he terms Gadamer's romantic claim that that we cannot transcend "the dialogue which we are" (253). Habermas maintains that philosophical hermeneutics is incomplete if it does not carry out a reflection on the limits of hermeneutic understanding. He seems to begin with the presupposition that hermeneutics is concerned with what enters everyday language in an undistorted manner. Thus, his own unexamined presuppositions enter into his interpretation of Gadamer's position. Yet, the question that he raises is important.

Habermas continues to raise the question of the relation of reason and language as he develops the example of psychoanalysis. But he also raises a further question. His question concerns the political implications of philosophical hermeneutics. He asks if Gadamer's rehabilitation of the concepts of prejudice and authority serve to perpetuate oppression rather than serving emancipation.

Habermas makes use of psychoanalysis to show that there are examples of "systematically distorted communication" (254). People involved in such distorted communication are not able to recognize that the communication is distorted. It takes the perspective of an external observer to recognize the distortion and to facilitate emancipation from the distortion. In the psychoanalytic setting, the therapist is the external observer who is in a position to facilitate healing such that open, or undistorted, communication can emerge. Habermas goes into detail in explaining the process of depth-hermeneutics that is used in the psychoanalytic situation. Habermas' point is that this is an example of a situation where inappropriate prejudices cannot be critiqued from within the lived experience of those in the situation. It takes an external understanding to call the internal interpretation into question and to lead to health. He does not view the analyst as a member of the conversation. The analyst functions as an external standard against which the hidden pathology can be revealed.

Psychoanalysis shows that consensus can be achieved within systems of distortion. There is the possibility of delusion in these systems without the possibility of overcoming that delusion. What a person believes to be true may be held to be true in order to cope or survive. The psychoanalyst presupposes a theory that takes certain communications, not at their face value, but as signs of hidden pathology. For communication to become free and undistorted requires the use of a theory of communicative competence.

Habermas believes that the example of psychoanalysis as depth-hermeneutics shows an instance where hermeneutical consciousness must reach beyond language and call on a standard, a rational regulative principle, outside of the situation in order to facilitate the movement towards truth. The example, according to Habermas, illustrates the independence of reason from language. He also thinks that the example of the psychoanalytic situation can be extended to social institutions. This extension of the example poses a more significant challenge to the claim of universality.

Habermas extends the psychoanalytic situation to the social setting. It is always possible, he maintains, that agreement that is achieved within communities may seem reasonable. But just as in the psychoanalytic setting, what seems reasonable to a person may actually be the result of pseudo-communication. The whole system of communication may be distorted such that structures of domination are perpetuated and not recognized. Any number of examples could be used to illustrate Habermas' point. When people are born into a system of slavery or other form of domination, they may actually accept their own domination as appropriate and see no need for emancipation. Habermas believes that Gadamer's philosophical hermeneutics cannot deal with this situation. If this criticism holds, it means that Gadamer's philosophical hermeneutics excludes the critique of much of human political life. It cannot serve political emancipation.

Habermas is particularly concerned with Gadamer's rehabilitation of the concept of authority. He believes that Gadamer has collapsed an important distinction between authority and reason. He writes, "Gadamer's argument presupposes that legitimizing recognition and the consensus on which authority is founded can arise and develop free from force" (269). Habermas thinks that the experience of distorted communication in both the psychoanalytic situation and in social structures challenges this presupposition. The implication of Habermas' position is that Gadamer is deluded in accepting authority as a positive presupposition for understanding. Habermas maintains that authority is really legitimated force, not legitimated knowledge. Gadamer's philosophical hermeneutics is limited and does not recognize its own limitations. What it needs is to recognize the need of hermeneutics for a principle of rational discourse so that the pathologies in social systems can be healed. For Gadamer to have the needed principle would require him to return to the Enlightenment distinction between authority and reason. Reason is the source of a standard of an idealized consensus achieved in communication free from domination.

Despite this criticism of Gadamer's work, Habermas does want to hold that humans cannot transcend the dialogue which we are. But what he means by this claim is very different from what Gadamer means. For Habermas, this means that criticism, which is the form of philosophical thought that he advocates, is always tied to and reflects tradition. Critique must always be aware of this and not be too hasty to claim a false universality. But the task of critique is to emancipate humans from the pathological aspects of tradition. Habermas assumes that the living tradition is dominated by these pathological aspects. It

60

produces social illness. Because of this assumption, Habermas is suspicious of the living tradition and of its ability to critique itself without the external standard of reason.

Gadamer's Response

Gadamer published "Reply to My Critics" in German in 1971. In this essay he responds to Habermas and others who challenged the universality of philosophical hermeneutics. He addresses Habermas' claim that reason is independent of human linguisticality. He also responds to Habermas' questions about the political implications of the use of the concept of authority. In responding to the political questions, he raises an important question to Habermas about the concept of emancipation. Finally, Gadamer discovers in this conversation with Habermas the importance of viewing hermeneutics as practical reasoning.

In response to Habermas' claim that science develops its own systems and so operates monologically, Gadamer simply states that while this is clearly the case, it is not a legitimate objection to philosophical hermeneutics. He remarks that,

> *Habermas, who raises this objection, knows himself that such 'understanding' and expertise (which constitute the pathos of modern social engineers and experts) lack precisely the kind of reflection which could give it social accountability.* (278)

Gadamer's point is that operating monologically does not constitute demonstration of science's independence from the whole of human lived experience. Indeed, Gadamer says that Habermas' use of psychoanalysis shows that science needs social reflection. Rather than function within the misconception that it is independent from the lived experience of daily life, science requires a hermeneutic reflection that will examine the presuppositions that it embodies. It is worth noting that Gadamer's position in this part of the discussion is supported by much contemporary work in current sociology of science.

Gadamer clearly understands the political concerns that are part of Habermas' questions and so devotes most of his reply to addressing these issues. He recognizes that Habermas' use of psychoanalysis presupposes that a social consciousness that agrees with a dominant social system actually supports its coercive character. This

61

consciousness is taken, by Habermas, to suffer from a social neurosis analogous to the neurosis of the individual patient. However, Gadamer maintains that "the relationship of social partnership is very different from that evident in the analytical relationship" (280). A simple example of this difference is that of telling a dream in the analytical situation and in the social situation. When a person recounts a dream in a social setting, there is no expectation that the dream will be interpreted by the listener in the context of a theory of resistance. The dream is not put forward for consideration for therapy. Gadamer offers another example. In a passionate political discussion where one person becomes angry with the other, what is expected is a counter-argument, not the analysis of the anger. Gadamer maintains that hermeneutic reflection is not intended as therapy. Rather than enable a person to cope in the social situation, hermeneutic reflection disturbs. Gadamer says, hermeneutic reflection "destroys self-understanding and reveals a lack of methodological justification" (281). Hermeneutical reflection is a process of on-going questioning.

In like manner, Gadamer maintains that effective-historical reflection is not aimed at actualization or bringing about application. He says, "To the contrary, its task is to impede and undermine all attempts to understand the tradition in terms of the most tempting, seductive opportunities which are being conceptualized" (282). Gadamer says that hermeneutic reflection is aimed at making every ideology suspect. The hermeneutic task is to decipher over and over again.

The ideal conditions that Habermas proposes are not possible. Gadamer emphasizes that the model of progress is not the appropriate model for hermeneutic research. He notes that philosophical hermeneutics does begin in the circumstances of concrete experience and that this includes "natural authority and the following which it finds" (287). Gadamer suggests that Habermas is exhibiting a dogmatic prejudice in assuming that what is operative in these concrete social structures will be found by reason to be coercive.

Gadamer gives several examples, including love and the choice of ideals. The language of love may be fairly stable in a society. Habermas seems to hold that when such forms of communication are stable in a society, that is indication that they are coercive. Habermas then holds that what is called for is emancipation. Gadamer is suspicious of this notion of emancipation. He suggests that the concept of emancipation, as Habermas uses it, presumes knowledge in the beginning rather than working to bring about agreement. He uses an example where he agrees with Habermas. Habermas claims that society's belief in experts is a superstition. Gadamer agrees with Habermas' insight, but not with Habermas' conclusion that what is called for is for society to free itself from this stage. Gadamer questions why the concept of emancipation requires a connection with the concept of stages. Habermas presupposes a type of development of human society in using the concept of stage that, to Gadamer, seems false (290).

Gadamer not only claims that Habermas has misunderstood the task of hermeneutical reflection. He also claims that Habermas has misunderstood what philosophical hermeneutics says about tradition. To recognize the importance of tradition is not to give preference to "that which is customary." He emphasizes, as he has already said in *Truth and Method,* that tradition "exists only in constantly becoming other than it is" (288). This is not a recognition of the truth of either revolutionary or conservative solidarity.

Continuing the Conversation

Some of Habermas' questions to Gadamer have to do with the relation of language and reason and others have to do with the political implications of Gadamer's thought. However, these questions are clearly connected. For Habermas, reason is a standard that stands against authority and that can measure the progress towards full emancipation. Gadamer does not think that political questions can be answered independently of their concrete situation. In that situation, agreement becomes the issue. Philosophical hermeneutics always asks if the presuppositions that are brought to the conversation that seeks agreement are dogmatic, or if they open understanding.

A contemporary example that deals with emancipation helps to clarify the issues at the heart of Habermas and Gadamer's conversation. Contemporary feminism seeks the emancipation of women. If Habermas is correct, then social structures can be shown to oppress women when the independent standard of reason is used against the authority of these social standards. Emancipation for women can occur by stages as reason develops steps of the critique of this domination. The concept of emancipation is presupposed, understood independently of the lived experience of women.

Gadamer does not directly address the role of women in society in his work, yet his responses to Habermas have much in agreement with contemporary feminism. While contemporary feminism certainly seeks the emancipation of women, the philosophical analysis that it has developed seems to support Gadamer more than Habermas. Feminism is sometimes accused of being ideological. This means that it is taken to presuppose a truth without being open to the critique of that position. While some feminists and some feminist position may be ideological in this sense, the feminist movement of the twentieth century more fully exemplifies Gadamer's position. Emancipation is not something that is grasped by reason independently of the concrete situation of women. Rather, feminism recognizes the importance of calling on the experience of women and of being critical of its own presuppositions. Feminism has developed as a philosophical approach that continually re-examines its concepts. It critiques its own presuppositions and develops an on-going conversation about the identity of feminism. The concepts that it uses to critique itself are not developed by reason independently of language. Rather, concepts are developed and used to help critique other concepts. In the course of this process, a space is opened for women that is more open and less oppressive. Emancipation occurs. But this is an on-going process. The concept of emancipation is constituted in language and is continually re-evaluated. It is worth remembering that this is the approach that Gadamer took in relation to Nazism during the Second World War. To preserve a space for free thought, the University, Gadamer chose to remain within the situation, doing as much as he could to challenge the self-understanding of the institutions so that a space for the pursuit of wisdom could be preserved.

While Gadamer believes that Habermas needs to reconsider the concepts of reason and emancipation that he uses, he does find Habermas' questions helpful. He writes, "the human good is something to be encountered in human *praxis*, and it is indeterminable without the concrete situation in which one thing is preferred to another." (293). Gadamer develops the insight that hermeneutics is *praxis*, practical philosophy. The exchange with Habermas is important in turning Gadamer's focus to a fuller articulation of how it is that hermeneutics is practical philosophy.

7

Practical Philosophy

Many of the essays that Gadamer publishes between 1976 and 1979 address the question of practice and what it means to recognize that hermeneutics is practical philosophy. *Reason in the Age of Science*, published in 1981, presents several of these essays in English translation. In these essays, Gadamer sets out more fully the task of authentically integrating science into human self-understanding in order to achieve a "new self-understanding of humanity." He writes of this new self-understanding,

> *We badly need this, for we live in a condition of ever-increasing self-estrangement, which, far from being caused by the peculiarities of the capitalist economic order alone, is due rather to the dependence of our humanity upon that which we have built around ourselves as our civilization.* (RAS 149)

Gadamer confirms and develops the position of *Truth and Method*. The task of philosophical hermeneutics is to enable humans to deal with the experience of alienation and to reflect on the knowledge that we have of ourselves. In reflecting on these issues in terms of practical philosophy, Gadamer is concerned with human freedom. In approaching hermeneutics as practical philosophy, he proposes to help humans develop the sort of self-knowledge that may enable us to recognize that we are dominated and dependent upon the very things that we believe we control.

Aristotle and Practice

Gadamer calls on the philosophical work of Aristotle to provide a foundation for understanding hermeneutics as practical philosophy. He suggests that Aristotle's concept of practical philosophy serves as a model for the type of fallible wisdom that characterizes human existence. Gadamer's approach of rehabilitating concepts by looking at their origins in tradition and then reflecting on these in relation to contemporary experience guides the beginning point of his reflections on hermeneutics as practical philosophy.

In explaining Aristotle's work, Gadamer stresses that Aristotle distinguished theoretical, practical, and productive sciences. Aristotle understood science in a very general manner. Science refers to any true knowledge. Science is knowledge of the universal that can be communicated or taught. Theoretical science, for Aristotle, refers to physics, mathematics, and theology. Practical science is concerned with the human good. It includes political philosophy and ethics. In Aristotle's thought theoretical and practical science are not in opposition with each other. Indeed, Aristotle views theoretical science as a practice. Moreover, practical science is concerned with universal principles of right action. However, Aristotle recognizes that some people may have knowledge of right action, of actions that will bring about human good, and not understand the principles embodied in those actions.

Gadamer focuses on two aspects of Aristotle's concept of practice. First, practice is "the mode of behavior of that which is living in the broadest sense" (RAS 90). In this most general sense, practice is a way of life. It is activity. In this general sense, all animals participate in practice. Humans, however, exhibit preferences and prior choices in their actions. Human practice involves choices among alternative possible actions. Secondly, these choices take place among free citizens in the *polis*, the Greek city-state. Human practice takes place in the context of open community.

Aristotle distinguishes practical science from productive science, or *techne*. In practical science, a person chooses freely, while productive science is a skill. Skills can be taught. Skills do not have to be accounted for in terms of their relationship to the good, but practical philosophy does. It chooses the good. Gadamer summarizes Aristotle's understanding of practical philosophy, "It must arise from practice itself and, with all the typical generalizations that it brings to explicit consciousness, be related back to practice" (RAS 92). Practical philosophy is like theoretical philosophy in that it seeks knowledge that is universal. But, it also is like productive science. Both the learner and the teacher must be involved in the concrete situation. But practical philosophy is distinct in that it focuses on the question of what is good. What is the best way to live? What is a good state? Good is not a private or individual concept, but a communal concept.

Science and Practice

Gadamer takes Greek philosophy as the foundation for most philosophical concepts. The Western tradition has its origins in the thought of Plato and Aristotle. These origins remain with us, even when they are concealed by later thought and concept development. However, Gadamer does not suggest that the Greeks always had the best understandings. He does think that looking at the origins or foundations of our concepts can sometimes enable us to reopen meaning that is contained within those concepts. When we live too closely to a concept, we may well overlook the richness and complexity of the concept. Interpretive distance enables us to understand the concept in a new way. This is the case with both science and practice.

In the essay, "What is Practice?" Gadamer maintains that contemporary science removes itself from the arena of the familiar world. It develops "into a knowledge of manipulable relationships by means of isolating experimentation" (RAS 70). This serves to tie science more closely to technology. Science furnishes the ideals that technology uses to construct things. Gadamer notes that through the medieval period, the user set the standard for what was made. The craftsperson made things according to the choice and decision of the user. But modern technology makes things and then "a consumer-awakening and need-stimulating industry is built around us" (RAS 71). Human choice is diminished in the building of our world. In addition, Gadamer says, we lose flexibility and freedom in relation to the world. We enjoy comforts, but we give up freedom.

The development of computer technology serves as an excellent example of Gadamer's analysis. Science continues to advance in the area of computer knowledge. As it advances, new technologies become possible. Computers and related software change more rapidly than those who use the technology on a daily basis can absorb. Users do not set the standards for this technology and have very little choice in relationship to the technology. As the technology develops, so does the market for the technology. We are convinced that we live in a world where we must be part of the technological age. And this is the case. Computers are pervasive. People place their trust in them. But it is also clear that computer technology places limits on human freedom. As computers become faster, work can be done more rapidly; but there is often also more stress. Sitting at a computer, a person may be expected to deal with electronic mail, phone conversations, paper mail, and electronic documents all at the same time. When the computer goes down, people may be unable to function.

Gadamer says that this relationship of science to technology in modern life has obscured concern for if and how work actually benefits people and for whether or not the achievements of technology actually serve life. Gadamer suggests that what has happened is "the degeneration of practice into technique and ... to a general decline into social irrationality" (RAS 74). He illustrates this claim with three examples.

Gadamer's first example of the collapse of the distinction between practical and productive science is the development and reliance on experts. He notes that more and more, contemporary Western societies include a pervasive expectation that we need planning. This seems to be a desire to have rational structure. While Gadamer wrote this in the 1970s, it may be even more the case in the 1990s. Institutions of all kinds adopt a model of planning that includes identifying missions, visions, and all sort of organizational processes. Gadamer points out that in the planning process, we turn to experts and expect these people to handle "practical, political, and economic decisions" (RAS 72). However, the expert really has the kind of knowledge that Aristotle termed *techne*. The expert has skills, but may not have the practical and political experiences that are necessary for practical knowledge. Yet, society expects the expert to determine the good for society. Despite the best intentions of the expert, he or she cannot fulfill the expectations of society.

In addition, Gadamer maintains that the twentieth century has undergone the "technologizing of the formation of public opinion" (RAS 73). At the end of the twentieth century, we use technology to deliver information. Technological media are some of the strongest forces in the shaping of public opinion. The forms that we use, like all forms of information delivery, require selection of information. Gadamer believes that this selection is done more and more for us. For example, television extracts fifteen seconds of information from much longer interviews. This information, along with the selection of images used, shape our understandings. Gadamer says, "It is inevitable, then, that the modern technology of communication leads to a more powerful manipulation of our minds" (RAS 73).

While contemporary humans may have an increase in information, Gadamer notes that this has not strengthened social reason. Often, the result of this technologizing of the delivery of information results in citizen apathy. People recognize that the information on political candidates is selected and screened for the impact on opinion. Because of this, there is a sense that there is no way to really know if a person is voting for the best candidate, or if any candidate is worthy of the public office. The result is apathy. Citizens do not participate in democracy because they see their vote as unimportant. Gadamer says that what also happens is "the elevation of adaptive qualities to privileged status" (RAS 73). What he means by this is that the social system rewards adaptability rather than creativity. Fewer people make decisions and more people are functionaries. They make society function, but they do not participate in the choices of what is best for society. According to Gadamer, this results even further in the loss of practical wisdom and its replacement with technique. Considerations of the human good do not enter into the choices related to human activities.

Gadamer believes that the connection between science and technology that includes the exclusion of practical science, has a catastrophic consequence for humans. This is the ecological crisis. He suggests that our experience does make us aware of this crisis. He says that we are aware that "a potential outgrowth of our economy and technology on the path that we have hitherto been treading is leading in the foreseeable future toward making life on this planet impossible" (RAS 84). If we can become aware of this, we can develop a solidarity. Certainly, this is a solidarity that develops out of necessity. We must preserve the planet in order to survive, but we can do this. What it requires is a rehabilitation of the concept of practice. We need to find ways of reconnecting the importance of what is good for humans to scientific development. We need to develop practical philosophy. Gadamer writes,

> *Practice is conducting oneself and acting in solidarity. Solidarity, however, is the decisive condition and basis of all social reason. There is a saying of Heraclitus, the "weeping" philosopher: The* logos *is common to all, but people behave as if each had a private reason. Does this have to remain this way?* (RAS 87)

Gadamer believes that it does not have to remain this way. Hermeneutics is the philosophical position that can provide contemporary humans with the needed philosophical position that can help people recognize the need to introduce considerations of the human good into all human actions, especially those that are directed by science.

Hermeneutics as Practical Philosophy

If hermeneutics is understood as practical philosophy, then it is that type of science that is concerned with human action and with the good for humans. Gadamer particularly emphasizes that hermeneutics as practical philosophy is characterized by its interest in questions, the endlessness of its task, and the recognition of the importance of communality.

Gadamer says that hermeneutics pushes people to go back to and examine the motivating questions behind all actions. It takes statements as answers to questions. Questions are motivated, and it is important to look for the motivation in the questions that influence human actions. As such, hermeneutics recognizes that our questions always reflect both conscious and unconscious motivations. Gadamer writes,

It is quite artificial to imagine that statements fall down from heaven and that they can be subjected to analytic labor without once bringing into consideration why they are stated and in what way they are the response to something. (RAS 107)

In examining questions, philosophical hermeneutics looks for the presuppositions that are embedded in those questions. In doing this, hermeneutics carries out the task of practical philosophy, by asking what humans take to be important in their lives. What people ask about gives indication of what they take to be important or of significance for their lives. Philosophical hermeneutics carries out an elaboration of what Gadamer calls the hermeneutic situation. It identifies the questions that people raise within the context of their lived experience. In identifying these questions, it also enables people to reflect on the appropriateness of those questions.

This task of examining questions is unending. Gadamer maintains that we can never fully understand the motivations and presuppositions of our questions. This is because the task of hermeneutics is not like that of psychoanalysis. The task of hermeneutics is not just to bring

70

unconscious presupposition to consciousness. Hermeneutics as practical philosophy also helps people understand vague presuppositions. It shows us that no matter how much we try to bring all presuppositions to light, some will always remain hidden. We can never bring everything to consciousness. Yet, Gadamer says, "it remains a legitimate task to clarify what lies at the basis of our interests as far as possible" (RAS 108).

Gadamer emphasizes that this task is not fundamentally a psychoanalytic task. He continues his conversation with Habermas in the course of explaining the task of philosophical hermeneutics. Gadamer maintains that psychoanalysis is at the limit, rather than the foundation, of the task of clarifying human interests. When the situation is one of complete concealment or distortion, Gadamer believes that psychoanalysis serves an important role. It enables an individual to regain equilibrium and so enter again into the conversation of the community. However, in most situations there is not such a breakdown of communication. Gadamer explains the task that philosophical hermeneutics carries out.

> *The task of understanding is not merely that of clarifying the deepest unconscious grounds motivating our interest but above all that of understanding and explicating them in the direction and limits indicated by our hermeneutic interest.* (RAS 108)

The realm of hermeneutic experience is the realm of shared meaning. The task of interest clarification takes place in conversation where people in community struggle to identify and act to bring about human good. Understanding is a type of action.

Gadamer suggests that, like other types of action, understanding always involves a degree of risk. He says that understanding is an adventure and so involves danger. Part of what it is to set out on an adventure is to be unsure as to what is going to happen and to know that there is potential for excitement and risk in what one is doing. When we enter into conversation with other people with the intent of identifying our presuppositions and letting our experiences challenge these presuppositions in order to better identify the good for human life, we risk our very existence. The structure of such conversations is like the structure of play that Gadamer developed in his analysis of aesthetic consciousness. Understanding is entering into play where we are not in control of the movement, but rather are changed by the play. Gadamer writes,

But when one realizes that understanding is an adventure, this implies that it afford unique opportunities as well. It is capable of contributing in a special way to the broadening of our human experiences, our self-knowledge, and our horizon, for everything understanding mediates is mediated along with ourselves. (RAS 110)

Carrying out the task of philosophical hermeneutics promises the possibility of the development of our individual self-understanding. It also promises the possibility of shaping and sharing in a common perspective or common language.

Gadamer emphasizes that that model for philosophical hermeneutics is conversation in which common language is discovered. When this happens, the participants are changed. He notes that this is a type of progress, but not a progress that can be measured in terms of stages. Again, he is continuing the discussion with Habermas. The sort of progress that takes place in conversation must be renewed and is a constant effort of life.

Gadamer concludes that what he has set out as philosophical hermeneutics is not a new methodology or technique. In some ways it is not anything new. "Basically it only describes what always happens wherever an interpretation is convincing and successful" (RAS 111). What philosophical hermeneutics does is call our attention to what happens when we understand. Theory and practice function reciprocally. We do not begin with a theory and apply it according to rules. It is more accurate to think that we begin in practice. We begin in a situation where we already understand. Our theoretical reflections on that situation are intended to make us aware of what is happening in the practical situation. Gadamer says, "This theoretic stance only makes us aware reflectively of what is performatively at play in the practical experience of understanding" (RAS 112). Philosophical hermeneutics is practical philosophy. It heightens our awareness of the experience of understanding. This awareness does not guarantee that right understanding will emerge, but it does contribute to the practice of understanding.

The Example of Health

In 1996 a collection of Gadamer's essays were published in English under the title, *The Enigma of Health*. The essays were written

72

over an eighteen year period between 1963 and 1991. The book serves as an excellent example of philosophical hermeneutics as practical philosophy. Many of these essays were written as presentations for groups of physicians and are quite accessible to a general reading public. They also address concerns about health which are certainly important for contemporary people, especially because,

> *We must take care of our own health through the way in which we lead our lives. This particular responsibility which each person bears expands into a much broader dimension of responsibility in our highly complex civilization.* (EH viii)

These essays exemplify the task of hermeneutics as practical philosophy. In the course of the essays contained in this volume, Gadamer acknowledges certain presuppositions that he brings to the analysis. He identifies the questions that motivate contemporary human concerns with the issue of health and follows the dynamic of those questions. He proposes aspects of self-understanding that are possible based on the examination.

Gadamer's Presuppositions

Gadamer's essays all presuppose the reflections on philosophical hermeneutics that he developed in *Truth and Method*. His concepts of horizon, effective-history, and play all enter into the approach that he takes to health. Most importantly, he begins with the presupposition that modern science is important and yet presents a challenge for human life and practice. He writes,

> *Knowledge, which can be transmitted independently of the situation of action and can thus be detached from the practical context of action, needs to be applied at times in a new situation of human action. Now the general empirical knowledge of human beings which decisively affects their practical decisions is inseparable from the knowledge which has been transmitted by specialized knowledge. What is more, it is an absolute moral duty to pursue knowledge to the greatest possible degree; that means today that one must also be informed by means of 'science.'* (EH 16)

This presupposition leads Gadamer to approach modern medicine as both a science and an art. It also leads him to bring his own question to the hermeneutic task. How do we integrate science more fully into human lives so that it serves the development of self-knowledge and human practice?

Motivating Questions

The title essay, "On the Enigmatic Character of Health," is particularly helpful for illustrating how Gadamer elucidates motivating questions. He suggests that addressing the broad range of questions that are associated with sickness and health will result in bringing "to light the fundamental tension which is particularly characteristic of our own scientifically grounded modern civilization" (EH 105).

The main question that Gadamer identifies as underlying medical science is the question: How can illness be mastered or controlled? He notes that medical science is really a science of illness. What concerns us is how to resist illness as something which resists us. This is the case for both the physician and the patient. The physician seeks to torture illness in order to drive it from the patient. The patient also seeks to drive illness from the body and regain control. When we approach health with this question, we overlook the significance of health. Gadamer says, "unfortunately, we are obliged to concede that the progress of science has been accompanied by a decline in our more general care for health and in preventative medicine in general" (EH 106). Asking a question that focuses on illness actually leads us to overlook health.

But when we identify and focus on the question that is asked, we do understand something about health. Gadamer says that we can understand that health is something that does not present itself to us. He says that health "sustains its own proper balance and proportion" (EH 107). Health cannot be measured. But part of the responsibility of medicine is to restore health. This is why medicine must be an art as well as a science. Physicians must not only fight illness, they must facilitate the process of a person becoming well, or whole. To help reestablish the equilibrium of health, the physician and the patient must both serve nature.

Gadamer looks at language usage to help illustrate how medicine needs to serve nature. We say that the physician treats or handles the patient. In German the word is *behandeln*. The physician makes use of touch to diagnose and treat a person. Learning to feel the body is an art that requires practice and the knowledge gained in this practice. To illustrate his point, Gadamer tells a story about a physician at Heidelberg, a Dr. Krehl. Gadamer relates that in 1920 the electric stethoscope was introduced. Students asked if this was an improvement over the earlier stethoscope. Krehl answered, "Well, the old stethoscopes were better for hearing with. But I cannot judge whether you have sufficient experience to benefit from them" (EH 109). For a physician, learning to treat a person requires hands-on experience.

Gadamer presses the concept of treatment. He notes that we speak of treating a person well or badly. If we treat a person well, we do not compel them. Gadamer says,

> *What is important is to recognize the other in their otherness, as opposed, for example, to the tendency towards standardization promoted by modern technology, the autocratic control of education by school authorities or the blind insistence on authority by a teacher or a father. Only by means of such recognition can we hope to provide genuine guidance which helps the other to find their own, independent way.* (EH 109)

The physician cannot control the patient and should not want to do this. The physician provides advice and is in the service of nature. The question of how to master illness leads to the realization that the physician must serve nature.

Emergent Self-Understanding

Gadamer began his reflections on health by suggesting that they would reveal a fundamental tension in human nature. The tension is that we are both in opposition to nature and sustained by nature. Gadamer says that we must recognize that "We can only oppose nature through being part of nature ourselves and through being sustained by nature" (EH 116).

For the patient/physician relationship, this means that health is not something that can be measured, but is a general feeling of well-being. Health is a condition of being involved and engaged in the world. Gadamer maintains that health is a state of equilibrium. Equilibrium is easily disturbed and so should not be adjusted without care. Anyone who has ever done a headstand can identify with this. When one is in balance or equilibrium the feeling of well-being is pervasive. However, the slightest adjustment of a foot or an elbow can send one tumbling to the ground. Similarly, the physician cannot control the rhythm or balance of the body.

Gadamer notes that "philosophers face the task of leading away from concrete things and yet, at the same time, bringing something genuinely illuminating to our attention" (EH 116). His reflections on health do not propose to give advice on specific medical processes or on healthcare systems. Yet, hermeneutics remains practical. It helps us arrive at fuller self-understanding. In the case of medical science, it helps us to recognize that medicine stands within the whole of life. Neither the physician nor the patient can fight illness without recognizing that the very nature that is battled is the nature that is to be sustained. This self-understanding can facilitate concrete choices that reduce domination, provide for well-being, and acknowledge the role of nature in recovery.

The self-understanding arrived at by means of Gadamer's reflections on health contribute to the self-understanding that hermeneutics develops. In particular, it continues to support Gadamer's emphasis that understanding takes place in language and is an activity of humans in community. Understanding is the task of developing language in which we can be at home.

8

Conversations

Although Gadamer chooses to remain quiet about himself as he develops his thinking, he emphasizes the centrality of dialogue or conversation for philosophy. His development of philosophical hermeneutics promotes the model of philosophy as authentic conversation. This book focuses on the development of his philosophical position and on one of the conversations that has been important for Gadamer's thinking. The conversation with Habermas has had important consequences for Gadamer's thought, contributing to the emphasis on practical philosophy.

Gadamer has, however, engaged in many conversations throughout his philosophical career. A brief presentation of several other of his conversations contributes to this general introduction to Gadamer's philosophical work. Some of these conversations have been with philosophers who preceded him. Plato, Aristotle, and Hegel have engaged Gadamer in thoughtful conversations that have informed and changed Gadamer's thought. Chapter Seven includes some indication of the importance of Aristotle for Gadamer. This chapter presents some of the important aspects of his conversations with Plato and Hegel. Other conversations have been with his contemporaries. Chapter One deals with some of those conversations. Because Heidegger has been a particularly important voice for Gadamer, some additional reflection on conversations with Heidegger is helpful. In addition, Gadamer has contributed to and his work has prompted conversations on numerous topics, including art and literature, the methodology of social science, and religion. A review of these on-going conversations completes this introduction. In keeping with Gadamer's approach, these conversations should be viewed as open-ended. We are invited to join in the conversations and be changed by them.

Conversations with Plato

Gadamer devoted much of his teaching career to Greek philosophy, especially the work of Plato (c. 428-347 BCE). His association with Heidegger helped him to find in Greek philosophy a way to approach philosophy that revitalized it. German philosophy, at the time that Gadamer began his career, was dominated by discussions of Kantian and Hegelian system-building. This approach to philosophy emphasizes grounding or providing foundation for all thought in some first principle. In Greek thought, Gadamer found a philosophical approach that emphasized the importance of basing philosophy on the fundamental experiences of human existence. In Greek philosophy, he also found an approach that emphasized that philosophy must be carried out in the "conceptual and intuitive power of the language in which we live" (Hahn 9). Philosophy cannot invent a language of its own, independent of the world of human lived experience.

Gadamer judges that the dialogues of Plato, perhaps more than any other philosophical work, have left their mark on his thinking. He particularly notes that "It is...Plato's dialogical art which serves as an antidote to the illusion of superiority which we think we possess as inheritors of the Judeo-Christian tradition" (Hahn 32). Gadamer learns from Plato the art of dialogue as an art that teaches us our own not-knowing, our ignorance. This means that in the course of conversation it dawns on us that we are living pretended knowledge. Plato's dialogue is not the development of argument or of a philosophical doctrine of ideas so much as it is the development of questions and a direction set by those questions. Gadamer says that Plato develops dialogue as the art of thinking and, "this means the art of seriously questioning what one really means when one thinks or says this or that. In doing so, one sets out on a journey, or better, is already on the journey" (Hahn 33-34). In reading and understanding Plato's work Gadamer comes to the conclusion that there is a natural human disposition towards philosophy. Plato provides a conversation partner with whom he develops most of the basic insights of his philosophical work.

A number of Gadamer's essays on Platonic philosophy are available to an English-reading audience. His essay "Plato and the Poets" is a good example of his conversations with Plato. This is the paper that he gave in 1933 for Bultmann's study group. It was published in 1934. The essay is an interpretation of Plato's *Republic* and Plato's decision to ban the poets from this State. It also serves as an indication of Gadamer's evaluation of National Socialism. It is prefaced by the quotation from Goethe, "Whoever philosophizes will not be in agreement with the conceptions of the times."

Gadamer begins this essay by telling the story of the young Plato who is reputed to have tried his hand at poetry by writing tragedies. When he met Socrates and became his disciple, he burned his plays. Gadamer proposes to look at Plato's decision to burn the tragedies and ask what this decision can mean for us. Gadamer suggests that Plato was not deciding that philosophy always takes priority over art. "Rather he recognizes that in the hour of his decision Socratic philosophy is not to be circumvented. And the poets fail just as much as anyone else to face up to this necessity" (DD 41). Gadamer reviews Plato's treatment of the relation of poetry and philosophy in many of the dialogues and concludes that Plato's position is a conscious decision. He writes of this decision that it was,

> *Made as a result of having been taken with Socrates and philosophy, made in opposition to the entire political and intellectual culture of his time, and made in the conviction that philosophy alone has the capacity to save the state.* (DD 47)

Gadamer reads Plato's placement of the critique of the poets in the *Republic* as demonstrating Plato's challenge to the foundations and the whole of the Greek tradition.

Gadamer interprets the purpose of Plato's state as developing what is right and just. This is needed in the time of Plato because poetry has been used to teach young people to value justice only for the advantages that it can bring. Poetry has been used to manipulate souls or as propaganda. While Gadamer is interpreting Plato and asking why he was so hard on the poets, he is clearly raising that question in light of the situation in Germany in 1933. Gadamer describes the justice that Plato seeks to help establish by writing the *Republic*. This description is not simply an historical account of Plato's position. He says,

> *What is just and right is not the right that someone has in*

79

opposition to another. Rather it is <u>being</u> just: Each <u>is</u> just by himself and all <u>are</u> just together. Justice does not exist when each person watches the other and guards against him but when each watches himself and guards the right and just being of his inner constitution. (DD 51)

Gadamer maintains that Plato banishes the poets to emphasize the need to purify the poetic tradition. Plato writes the *Republic* to awaken the Greek people to what is needed to create a just state. It should not be understood as a political model to be followed with authority. Rather, the *Republic* serves to motivate people to raise questions. As people learn to raise questions, they will discover the justice in their own souls and so become more just political people. This is all a prelude to the formation of just laws by the people.

Gadamer's essay develops an extensive interpretation of the *Republic* that supports his claim. This essay is worth reading in relation to the *Republic*, as an insight into the historical times and how some intellectuals dealt with the political times, and as an insight into the development of Gadamer's philosophical hermeneutics. In relation to the development of philosophical hermeneutics, this essay demonstrates the beginnings of Gadamer's later emphasis on the importance of practical philosophy. Philosophy begins with choices and is concerned with the good for human existence. The essay also shows the beginnings of Gadamer's emphasis on conducting dialogue as open-ended. Authentic conversation, conversation that enables individuals and communities to live justly, must be guided by questions. It must recognize that thinking is never complete.

Conversations with Hegel

Georg Wilhelm Friedrich Hegel (1770-1831) developed dialectic with the goal of a total and complete system. Hegel's concept of the dialectical movement of experience is closely connected to the Platonic emphasis on dialogue. Gadamer's interest in dialogue and his historical situation, living at a time when much of German philosophy was developing in relation to Hegel's thought, required him to wrestle with Hegel's understanding of dialectic. He writes of Hegel that his "dialectic is a continual source of irritation" (HD 3).

Gadamer finds insight in Hegel, and yet is constantly in disagreement with Hegel's movements towards completeness. He believes that Hegel's insistence on totality and infinity close dialogue rather than recognizing the unending character of all dialectic or dialogue. Hegel's work irritates Gadamer because it is both so insightful and so misleading. For example, Hegel develops the insight that is present in Plato's dialogues. Philosophy must always include "that anticipation of the whole which lies imbedded in language as the totality of our access to the world" (HD 3). Yet, Hegel claims that this dialectic is a process of clear demonstration. Furthermore, Hegel proposes to move philosophy beyond a philosophy of consciousness that emphasizes the dichotomy of subject and object. However, he is unable to embrace human existence in its finitude.

In struggling with Hegel's thought, Gadamer is challenged to reflect on these issues. While Gadamer does not come to agree with Hegel, his conversations with Hegel illustrate the importance of thinking with those whose thought challenges. Gadamer comes to view his own work as restoring Hegel's notion of "bad infinity" to a more honorable position. For Hegel, thinking is infinite because it continually moves beyond every limit. The bad infinite appears to be infinite, but is really determined by something that is beyond it. Gadamer takes the challenge to think that which is limited and yet open.

Gadamer's essay "Hegel's Dialectic of Self-consciousness" illustrates this approach to his conversations with Hegel. He makes use of Hegel to develop contemporary conversations without accepting Hegel's complete system. This essay, published in 1973, comes forty years after the essay on Plato. It demonstrates Gadamer's continued emphasis on the importance of returning to texts of the tradition and letting them speak to us in our contemporary situation. In this essay, Gadamer carries out a very careful reading of chapter 4 of Hegel's *Phenomenology of Spirit*. In this very famous chapter, Hegel develops what is often referred to as the Master/Slave dialectic. This section of Hegel's work was used by Marx is his analysis of the relationship of the bourgeois and the proletariat. Gadamer's reading shows the importance of this section of the *Phenomenology* for Hegel's development of an understanding of human freedom. Gadamer believes that this section is best read by suspending Marx's interpretation. Gadamer notes that Hegel was not describing wage work, but farm work and handwork.

This essay is clearly written and is an excellent aid in reading Hegel's work. It also illustrates how Gadamer suggests that we need to think in relationship to the philosophical thought of our tradition. In reading Hegel, Gadamer is developing the conversation on freedom that motivated much of Hegel's thought. In reading this particular passage, Gadamer emphasizes Hegel's treatment of the fear of death as our ultimate Master. Gadamer's thought is clearly influenced by Heidegger's concept of human existence as a being-towards-death. However, in reading Hegel as he does, Gadamer emphasizes that freedom is not just a confirmation of a self given to us, but it is also "successful self-assertion in opposition to dependency on existent things" (HD 70). In facing death and in work, we are able to recognize ourselves as free of dependency on material things. Gadamer concludes, that if Marx is correct in the analysis that work in an industrialized society does not permit a worker to find significance, we must ask who can be free. In industrial society, we become consumers and are coerced by things. The truth that Gadamer finds in Hegel is the claim that "if there is to be freedom, then first of all the chain attaching us to things must be broken" (HD 74). Gadamer's point is that prosperity, having material things, is not necessarily a path to freedom. When freedom is understood as self-understanding, both individually and as a community, universal prosperity may well result in domination, not freedom. Gadamer's reading of Hegel takes the conversation on human freedom and shows that it is still an open question that addresses us. In doing this, Gadamer challenges Hegel's total system, but makes use of the richness of Hegel's thought.

Conversations with Heidegger

Of all of the thinkers who have engaged Gadamer, Martin Heidegger (1889-1976) has most stimulated Gadamer's thought and, perhaps, most closely shared the direction of Gadamer's own thought. Gadamer tells the story of how he first learned of Heidegger. In Munich in 1921 a student spoke passionately after a seminar using language that seemed very strange to Gadamer. When Gadamer asked the instructor of the class about this language, he received the response, "Oh that. He has been Heideggerized" (HW 113). It would not be accurate to say that Gadamer was also "Heideggerized." Gadamer's contact with Heidegger confirmed thoughts that were already taking shape for him. While it is possible to understand Gadamer's work as dependent upon and developing out of Heidegger's work, it is probably more accurate to see the two as walking similar paths or taking similar journeys. As these paths continually crossed and merged, Heidegger's though served to confirm for Gadamer the importance of the direction in which his own thought was moving.

Gadamer's memorial address, "Being Spirit God," given after Heidegger's death, illustrates his deep understanding of and sympathy with Heidegger's task. He says of Heidegger, "the passion of thinking made him quake – stirred as much by the force exerted on him by this passion as by the boldness of the questions that this passion compelled him to ask" (HW 182). Gadamer's address traces Heidegger's philosophical journey. In this account of Heidegger's path, Gadamer's path is also illumined.

Gadamer maintains that Heidegger's thought began with the question: How can one speak of God? Heidegger was concerned to raise this question without reducing God to an object of human knowledge. Heidegger found that he could not ask this question as a theologian without falling into misunderstanding. What was needed was to figure out what questions needed to be asked in order to ask this question about God. So Heidegger was led to ask what the long philosophical tradition of western metaphysics has meant by Being. To address the question of God required Heidegger to set out on a philosophical journey.

Gadamer suggests that Heidegger's thinking in *Being and Time* was "preliminary preparation for the question of Being." While Heidegger's work is often read as a rejection of metaphysics, Gadamer finds that "The question breaking forth in Heidegger's thought experiments allows the answer of metaphysics to speak anew" (HW 185). Gadamer believes that what Heidegger did in overcoming metaphysics was to battle against the resistance of language. Heidegger needed to find articulation in concepts while trying to avoid the concepts of metaphysics and all of the objectifying understanding that they contain. So, Heidegger began pushing the limits of concepts and finding concepts in places such as Friedrich Hölderlin's poetry and in works of art.

Heidegger struggled with language in order to try to help humans be at home in the world. Gadamer says that Heidegger found in Hölderlin's work hope that "the dialogue of thinking can still find a partner" even when faced with the remoteness of the divine. He concludes, "And the dialogue continues, for only in a dialogue can a language arise and continue to develop – a language in which we, in a more and more estranged world, are at home" (HW 195).

Gadamer is not simply a disciple of Heidegger. Indeed, Gadamer never adopted many of the concepts that Heidegger developed in his thought. Other essays on Heidegger's thought by Gadamer show Gadamer's differences with Heidegger more clearly. This address presents Heidegger in a more Gadamerian light that Heidegger would have liked. Yet, the address demonstrates how important conversation with Heidegger has been for the articulation of Gadamer's own philosophical journey.

On-going Conversations

Gadamer's philosophical hermeneutics has contributed to the thinking of many contemporary philosophers. Those who have worked most closely with him and who continue the work of philosophical hermeneutics acknowledge the conversational community that Gadamer has facilitated by his work and his personal example. Conversations inspired by his thinking continue to develop in many areas. For example, the conversation with Plato concerning hermeneutics and politics is continued by Fred Dallmayr in "Hermeneutics and Justice," an essay that he contributes to Kathleen Wright's edited volume, *Festivals of Interpretation.* Dallmayr maintains that in our era of mass culture, Gadamer's reading of Plato reminds us of the importance of portraying violence as violence rather than as routine behavior, corruption as corruption rather than as the way of the world, and suffering as suffering rather than as unavoidable. He suggests that Gadamer's hermeneutics can help us avoid self-indulgence and apathy.

It is not possible in this general introduction to Gadamer's philosophy to deal with all of the on-going conversations in detail. In addition to the conversations that have been introduced, three conversations are significant for the contemporary task of philosophical thought. His work on aesthetic consciousness and on literary texts continues to be important to conversations in the areas of aesthetics and literary interpretation. Conversations that are indebted to his thought are taking place in the social sciences. His work also has contributed to conversations on religion. All of these conversations are on-going. In keeping with Gadamer's belief that we are all philosophers at heart, the following introductions to these conversations are meant as invitations to join in the task and conversations of philosophical hermeneutics.

Aesthetics and Hermeneutics

In addition to the reflections on aesthetics that Gadamer developed in the first section of *Truth and Method*, he has written many essays on art. Many of these are available in English in *The Relevance of the Beautiful*, edited by Robert Bernasconi. These essays elaborate on many of the concepts developed in *Truth and Method*, especially the concepts of play, symbol, and festival. He shows how each of these concepts provides self-understanding, showing us our experience of participating in something greater that ourselves while we are also involved in constructive activity. He develops his understanding of art as showing us our finitude, especially our possibilities for constructing and preserving meaning. He writes,

> *The work of art provides a perfect example of the universal characteristic of human existence - the never-ending process of building a world. In the midst of a world in which everything familiar is dissolving, the work of art stands as a pledge of order.*
> (RB 103-4)

Gadamer's discussion of art is carried out with his conversations with Hegel in the background. He contends that we should not expect art to provide complete self-understanding, nor should we expect aesthetic experience to replace religious experience.

In *Truth and Method*, Gadamer emphasizes the importance of works of art that are literary and the task of hermeneutics as carrying out conversations with texts. Many of the conversations that have emerged out of this aspect of his work have focused on issues of textual interpretation. In 1981, a particularly important conversation began. Gadamer and Jacques Derrida both presented papers at a Paris colloquium. Derrida's work in literary theory, known as deconstruction, is also extremely important for contemporary philosophy and has had considerable impact in many areas of contemporary thought.

The papers presented by Gadamer and Derrida and the ensuing conversation are available in *Dialogue and Deconstruction*, edited by Dianne Michelfelder and Richard Palmer. In the two presentations, it is clear that Gadamer and Derrida have different understandings of interpretation. In Gadamer's reply to Derrida, he admits to having difficulty in understanding some of Derrida's questions. Yet, he writes, "I believe I am not very far from Derrida when I stress that one never knows in advance what one will find oneself to be" (57). Gadamer recognizes in Derrida's thought the attempt to understand human finitude. This conversation is being continued by many voices asking the question: How is it that the language of philosophy and the language of poetry belong together and yet diverge? While this conversation may seem to be primarily an academic conversation, the implications for human self-understanding and community are significant. If it is the case that philosophy and literature and the conversation between the two help us to understand who we are, then marginalizing these activities and texts within our society also serves to inhibit our own possibilities of self-understanding.

Social Science and Hermeneutics

The conversation between Gadamer and Habermas has precipitated much interesting and important conversation about social science and hermeneutics. These discussions are predominately concerned with the role of theory, particularly theories of communication and social evolution. Some of these conversations are closely tied to the thought of Habermas and/or Gadamer. Others develop the conversation about hermeneutics and social science at a distance from, and yet in contact with the Gadamer/Habermas conversation. Many conversations are concerned with what it means to develop an interpretive sociology.

Anthony Giddens is an important voice in the conversation as it is carried on in the social sciences. Giddens has written numerous books, engaging a wide range of thinkers in his reflections on the relation of social science and hermeneutics. His essay, "Hermeneutics and Social Theory" in *Hermeneutics, Questions and Prospects*, edited by Gary Shapiro and Alan Sica, provides a helpful starting point for joining this conversation. In this essay, Giddens summarizes his work in developing what he terms a theory of structuration and also develops a 'double hermeneutic.' The first part of this hermeneutic relies on Weberian sociology and interprets social action using concepts of forces, needs, intentions, and cultural processes. The second part of the hermeneutic looks at language used in theory as itself a human construction. While Giddens does not work out of Gadamer's analysis of the task and development of hermeneutics, his work is clearly influenced by the conversations begun by Gadamer and continues to follow the question: How can situated humans understand themselves in community and understand how to build human community?

Religion and Hermeneutics

Søren Kierkegaard (1813-1855), the critic of Hegel and founding thinker of contemporary existentialism, developed indirect communication as a way of talking about the infinite from the perspective of human finitude and so of more fully understanding human finitude. Gadamer identifies Heidegger's motivating question: How can one speak of God? He also notes that Heidegger finds that this question can only be addressed indirectly. While it is Heidegger's philosophical thought that has most influenced contemporary conversations about religion and hermeneutics, Gadamer's thought also begins with and continually returns to the fundamental importance of religious experience and concepts. Gadamer's motivating question is like that of Kierkegaard and Heidegger. He too, takes an indirect path in order to avoid forcing an answer upon the question: How is it possible for finite humans to experience the infinite?

In *Truth and Method*, Gadamer makes use of many religious concepts as he develops philosophical hermeneutics. As Chapter 5 shows, the concept of the Incarnation is particularly significant for his work. Gadamer also relies on the I-Thou relationship as developed first by Kierkegaard and later by the Jewish theologian, Martin Buber. He uses this concept to help describe how tradition is encountered in hermeneutical experience. The I-Thou relationship includes a moral experience where one is engaged in a living relationship with the Thou. The Thou is known as a person in that living relationship. The Thou is not an object of knowledge. In fact, if the Thou is thought as an object, the moral bond is destroyed and so is the I-Thou relationship is also dissolved. This relationship is reflected in everyday language use. When we say that we understand someone, we mean that we are engaged by their lives and that they are recognized as persons who can give or withhold themselves from our knowledge and understanding.

The concept of the I-Thou relationship is not analyzed by Gadamer in order to address theological issues, yet it is apparent that his use of this and other religious concepts proclaims the importance of religious experience for all human experience. Religious experience takes the form of the I-Thou relationship and so reveals how fundamentally human experience is engaged and relational. It also emphasizes the importance of language for this engaged connection.

Another example of the importance of religious concepts, especially Christian concepts, for Gadamer's thought is in the essay "Aesthetic and Religious Experience" which is translated in *The*

Relevance of the Beautiful. Again, Gadamer is not making any attempt to do theology. Yet, he reflects on what it means to say that the gospel is freely offered. He writes,

> *If the Christian message does represent such a freely made offer, a free promise, which is directed at each of us although we have no claim on it, then the task of proclaiming it is implied by our acceptance of it.* (RB 148)

Proclamation is not simply a repetition of the message. It requires that the message be proclaimed in a way that it can actually reach people. The understanding belongs to the communication of the message. Gadamer describes the missionary task of Christianity as following from this realization of the nature of proclamation. Gadamer is not advocating colonial missionary zeal. The message of the gospel, he says, is not like that of art. Art can show us, to our amazement and horror, what we can achieve. The Christian message, he says, "shows what we cannot achieve" (RB 153).

In 1994, Gadamer was invited to participate in a conversation on religion that took place on Capri with Derrida, Gianni Vattimo, and several others. The conversation was motivated by the question: Is religious revival really anything other than the death of God? This discussion clearly developed within the influence of Heidegger's thought. "Dialogues in Capri" is Gadamer's essay that contributes to the record of the conversation, *Religion, Cultural Memory in the Present*, edited by Derrida and Vattimo. Gadamer emphasizes the need to open this discussion to other participants, especially women and people from non-European religious traditions. Religious experience cannot be considered if it is not approached in its full global perspective.

Yet, Gadamer suggests that there is one thing that is never absent from religious experience, "the knowledge of one's own death and at the same time the impossibility of the actual experience of death" (205). This he says, shows us something of what it is to be human. As humans we have knowledge of our own limit or end. Gadamer calls on Greek tragedy to develop this claim. Aeschylus wrote the story of Prometheus as the one who disguises from humans the day and hour of their death. Gadamer writes,

> *What we learn from the play is that the impenetrable mystery and uncanniness of death accompanies, like a dowry, that capacity to conceive the future which distinguishes human beings from other*

living creatures, and that this is a dangerous gift. It seems that, in anticipating what is to come, we are irresistibly led to try to think beyond the certainty of death. (206)

Gadamer connects the attempt to think beyond death with language and suggests that the two are inseparable. Each allows something to be brought before us in its absence. The task of humanity is to live in openness towards this end.

The Quiet Word

Gadamer's work serves to motivate many conversations. In joining these conversations, we are well advised to remember Gadamer's emphasis upon quietness. The twentieth century has been a period in which humans have been faced with the exciting and horrifying possibilities of our existence. In "Are the Poets Falling Silent" Gadamer suggests that what is most needed in our time are quiet words. He writes, "only the quietest word still confirms the communality and therefore, the humanity, which you and I find in the word." Both the speaker and the listener must be attentive to such words. Gadamer concludes the essay with the question,

And who will determine which experiences of skillfulness reach out from the life of technical civilization into these word constructions and are captured in them, so that we are able to suddenly meet and welcome, in this our house, the powerful foreignness of the modern world as something familiar? (EPH 81)

Glossary and List of
Abbreviations

Glossary

Geisteswissenschaften--human sciences or humanities
hören--hearing
Sachlichkeit--factualness
Spiel--play
Sprachlichkeit--linguisticality; the linguistic condition of understanding
Überlieferung--tradition
Vorurteil--prejudice
Wirkungsgeschichte--effective-history
Zeitenabstandes--temporal distance
Zugehörigkeit--belongingness

List of Abbreviations

DD	*Dialogue and Dialectic*
EH	*The Enigma of Health*
EPH	*Hans-Georg Gadamer on Education, Poetry, and History*
HW	*Heidegger's Ways*
PA	*Philosophical Apprenticeships*
PH	*Philosophical Hermeneutics*
RB	*The Relevance of the Beautiful*
RAS	*Reason in the Age of Science*
TM	*Truth and Method*

Bibliography

English Translations of Gadamer's Writing

Dialogue and Dialectic: Eight Hermeneutical Studies on Plato. Trans. P.
  Christopher Smith. New Haven, CN: Yale UP, 1980.
The Enigma of Health: The Art of Healing in a Scientific Age. Trans. Jason
  Gaiger and Nicholas Walker. Stanford, CA: Stanford UP, 1996.
*Hans-Georg Gadamer on Education, Poetry, and History: Applied
  Hermeneutics.* Ed. Dieter Misgeld and Graeme Nicholson. Trans.
  Lawrence Schmidt and Monica Reuss. Albany, NY: SUNY Press, 1992.
Hegel's Dialectic: Five Hermeneutical Studies. Trans. P. Christopher Smith.
  New Haven, CN: Yale UP, 1976.
Heidegger's Ways. Trans. John W. Stanley. Albany, NY: SUNY Press, 1994.
The Idea of the Good in Platonic-Aristotelian Philosophy. Trans. P.
  Christopher Smith. New Haven, CN: Yale UP, 1986.
Literature and Philosophy in Dialogue: Essays in German Literary Theory.
  Trans. Robert H. Paslick. Albany, NY: SUNY Press, 1994.
Philosophical Apprenticeships. Trans. Robert R. Sullivan. Cambridge: MIT
  Press, 1985.
Philosophical Hermeneutics. Trans. David E. Linge. Berkeley: U of
  California P, 1976.
Reason in the Age of Science. Trans. Frederick G. Lawrence. Cambridge:
  MIT Press, 1981.
The Relevance of the Beautiful and Other Essays. Ed. Robert Berasconi.
  Trans. Nicholas Walker. Cambridge: Cambridge UP, 1986.
Truth and Method. Second Edition Trans. Revised Joel Weinsheimer and
  Donald G. Marshall. New York: Crossroad, 1992.

Books and Anthologies

Bernstein, Richard J. *Beyond Objectivism and Relativism.* Philadelphia: U
  of Pennsylvania P, 1983.

91

Bleicher, Josef. *Contemporary Hermeneutics.* London: Routledge & Kegan Paul, 1980.

DiCenso, James. *Hermeneutics and the Disclosure of Truth: A Study in the Work of Heidegger, Gadamer, and Ricoeur.* Charlottesville: UP of Virginia, 1990.

Derrida, Jacques and Gianni Vattimo. *Religion, Cultural Memory in the Present.* Stanford, CA: Stanford UP, 1996.

Grondin, Jean. *Introduction to Philosophical Hermeneutics.* New Haven, CN: Yale UP, 1994.

Hahn, Lewis Edwin, ed. *The Philosophy of Hans-Georg Gadamer.* Chicago: Open Court, 1997. (Contains Gadamer's Autobiography)

Howard, Roy J. *Three Faces of Hermeneutics.* Berkeley, CA: U of California P, 1982.

Hoy, David Couzens. *The Critical Circle.* Berkeley, CA: U of California P, 1982.

Kresic, Stephanus, ed. *Contemporary Literary Hermeneutics and Interpretation of Classical Texts.* Ottawa: Ottawa UP, 1981.

Madison, G. B. *The Hermeneutics of Postmodernity.* Bloomington, IN: Indiana UP, 1988.

Michelfelder, Diane P. and Richard E. Palmer, eds. *Dialogue and Deconstruction, The Gadamer-Derrida Encounter.* Albany, NY: SUNY Press, 1989. (Contains five essays by Gadamer)

Ormiston, Gayle L. and Alan D. Schrift, eds. *The Hermeneutic Tradition.* Albany, NY: SUNY Press, 1990.

Palmer, Richard. *Hermeneutics.* Evanston, IL: Northwestern UP, 1969.

Schmidt, Lawrence K. *The Epistemology of Hans-Georg Gadamer.* Frankfurt: Peter Lang, 1985.

Shapiro, Gary and Alan Sica, eds. *Hermeneutics, Questions and Prospects.* Amherst, MA: U of Massachusetts P, 1984.

Silverman, Hugh J., ed. *Gadamer and Hermeneutics.* New York: Routledge, 1991.

Smith, P. Christopher. *Hermeneutics and Human Finitude: Toward a Theory of Ethical Understanding.* New York: Fordham Press, 1991.

Sullivan, Robert. *Political Hermeneutics: The Early Thinking of Hans-Georg Gadamer.* University Park, PA: Penn State UP, 1990.

Wachterhauser, Brice R., ed. *Hermeneutics and Modern Philosophy.* Albany, NY: SUNY Press, 1986.

Warnke, Georgia. *Gadamer: Hermeneutics, Tradition, and Reason.* Stanford: Stanford UP, 1987.

Weinsheimer, Joel C. *Gadamer's Hermeneutics: A Reading of Truth and Method.* New Haven, CN: Yale UP, 1985.

Wolff, Janet. *Hermeneutic Philosophy and the Sociology of Art.* London: Routledge & Kegan Paul, 1975.

Wright, Kathleen, ed. *Festivals of Interpretation.* Albany, NY: SUNY Press, 1990.